Exploring the Bible
THE DICKINSON SERIES

WHAT IS THE BIBLE?

Leader's Guide Large Print Edition
Second Edition

Rev. Anne Robertson

Foreword by Exploring the Bible benefactor,
Dr. Charles C. Dickinson, III

MASSACHUSETTS BIBLE SOCIETY
One Book, Many Voices

Copyright © June 2013 by the Massachusetts Bible Society
Copyright © 2nd Edition 2014

All rights reserved. No part of this book may be reproduced, stored in a retrieval system, or transmitted in any form or by any means, electronic, mechanical, including photocopying, recording, or otherwise, without the written permission of the publisher.

Unless otherwise indicated, Bible quotations in this book are from the New Revised Standard Version Bible, copyright © 1989 by the National Council of Churches of Christ in the U.S.A. Used by permission. All rights reserved.

Massachusetts Bible Society
199 Herrick Road,
Newton Centre, MA 02459

Book design by Thomas Bergeron
www.thomasbergeron.com
Typeface: Jenson Pro, Gill Sans

ISBN-13: 978-0-9907212-6-0
2ND EDITION

To Dr. Charles C. Dickinson
who, through his generosity, has given the Massachusetts Bible Society the opportunity to expand the knowledge of the Bible in ways that would not have been possible without his support.

TABLE OF CONTENTS

Acknowledgments

Welcome
Introducing <u>Exploring the Bible: The Dickinson Series</u>	iii
Our Theological Point of View	ix
Course Administration	ix

Leading Exploring the Bible: The Dickinson Series
Your Students	xi
Your Class	xix
You Are a Facilitator	xxii
Becoming a Registered Group Leader	xxvii

Overview of Class Session Elements
Check-In	xxix
Bible Activity	xxx
Life Connection Activity	xxxi
Review of Homework	xxxi
Extra Mile Presentations	xxxii
First and Last Sessions	xxxiii

Lesson Plans
Session 1: Orientation To The Bible	1
Session 2: Choosing A Bible	17
Session 3: Overview Of The Old Testament	27
Session 4: Overview Of The New Testament	33
Session 5: The Bible And Its Authority	41
Session 6: Archaeology And The Bible	55

Forms, Handouts, And Supplemental Material
Form: Student Evaluation	65
Form: Facilitator Evaluation	71
Massachusetts Bible Society Statement on Scripture	75
A Covenant for Bible Study	76
Session 1 Handout: Class Contact Information	77
Session 1 Handout: I Heard It in the Bible	79
Session 2 Handout: Stumbling Blocks	81
Sample Advertising Blurbs for <u>What Is the Bible?</u>	83
Glossary from Student Text	84

Acknowledgments

So many people have played a role in bringing this first course of <u>Exploring the Bible: The Dickinson Series</u> to life. Of course there is Dr. Dickinson, himself, to whom I have dedicated this first course; but there are also many others.

First there are the Trustees of the Massachusetts Bible Society who were willing to take a chance on this vision and allow me the time to develop the materials. From their editorial input, to their moral support, to their willingness to pilot classes in their communities, their engagement has been critical to making this a successful program.

Special thanks are also due to the parishes and leaders that piloted the course in their communities: First Parish Church in Weston, Massachusetts; First Unitarian Society in Newton, Massachusetts; Lutheran Church of the Newtons in Newton Centre, Massachusetts; Sacred Heart Parish in Middleboro, Massachusetts; and St. Matthew's United Methodist Church in Acton, Massachusetts. Their feedback and willingness to work with unfinished materials allowed us to be absolutely certain that our finished product was worthy of your time and resources.

Of course the staff of the Massachusetts Bible Society: Jocelyn Bergeron, Mike Colyott, and Frank Stevens provided the backbone for the work. They handled logistics for facilitator training and pilot courses, hunted for illustrations, and picked up the many tasks that were flying off of my plate as I concentrated on this. They kept me on track and on budget and kept me sane. There is not a more awesome staff anywhere.

Finally, I am extremely grateful to editor Nancy Fitzgerald, copyeditor Jennifer Hackett, proofreader Maria Boyer, and designer Thomas Bergeron who took a rough diamond and made it shine. They have made my life so much easier and have provided creative and helpful input all along the way.

In Gratitude,

Anne Robertson

Welcome

The Bible. Just hearing the word makes some people sing and other people cringe. For some it conjures up images of crusades and inquisitions and preachers shaking their fists at unrepentant sinners. For others it evokes feelings of comfort, joy, and warm memories of Sunday School songs and church pageants. Still others respond with an eye to the culture, recognizing the hole that would be left in art, architecture, music, and literature without the rich base of stories and imagery in the pages of the Bible.

So what's the deal? How does the person who would like to find out more about the Bible navigate that sea of conflicting ideas, emotions, and interpretations? How do you even stick your toe in those waters without drowning or being led so far from shore that you can't find your way back?

Well, it just so happens that we have this set of courses…

Introducing Exploring the Bible: The Dickinson Series

Exploring the Bible: The Dickinson Series is a series of three, six-week courses that leads to a Certificate in Biblical Literacy from the historic Massachusetts Bible Society.

Each of the three courses is designed to fit six ninety-minute sessions with a group of eight to fifteen people. The Massachusetts Bible Society provides training, materials, and ongoing support for those who would like to run the program in their local churches or communities. Those leading the courses are not expected to be biblical experts or pastors. They are those gifted and trained to facilitate a warm, welcoming, and open group environment where the material can be presented and discussed with respect for all participants.

The Exploring the Bible Program

Three Courses: A Bird's-Eye View

I. **What Is the Bible?** A broad overview of the Bible, including chapters on how to select a Bible suitable for your needs, how the Bible is organized, how the collection of books that comprise the Bible were chosen, different ways that people approach the text, and what archaeology has to tell us about the text and its stories.

II. **Introducing the Old Testament.** A look at the best-known stories, most influential passages, and unforgettable characters that comprise the Old Testament. What are the primary themes and narratives? What are the characteristics of ancient Hebrew literature and the mindset of people in the ancient Near East? Explore both the writings themselves and the historical contexts that gave them birth.

III. **Introducing the New Testament.** Learn about Jesus as a man, as a Jewish rabbi, and as the Christ of Christian faith. Explore first-century Nazareth, what ancient letter-writing practices can tell us about Paul's letters, and the wild apocalypse of Revelation.

Online Resources

Join us for discussion on the Exploring the Bible Facebook page and follow us on Twitter @ExploreBible and swap questions and experiences with others across the country and across the world who are doing the courses in their local communities. Many of you are asking for the opportunity to take the courses online and we hope to be able to offer that down the road. And you can always check out our website at exploringthebible.org for other news, recommended reading, and to find a course near you.

The Exploring the Bible Students

The series is designed for two distinct types of students:

The Casual or Informal Students. The first group is made up of those who might know something about the Bible but have gaps in their knowledge, or those who just want to test the waters of biblical studies. These students might want simply to take one of the three courses or put together some combination of those components without doing all that is necessary to complete the certificate program. While it's expected that this second group will still actively participate in whatever course(s) they select, there is less work expected of them outside the group setting.

The Intentional or "Extra Mile" Students. The second group represents those who have determined that they really want to do some work to build a strong foundation for Bible study. They might be Christians considering seminary, people of faith who don't know their own Scriptures very well, people of other faiths who want a clearer understanding of the Christian text, or even people of no faith who recognize the cultural and geopolitical influence of the Bible and want to understand it better. The common denominator among this group is that they want to do the whole program, including the "Extra Mile" assignments required to earn the Certificate of Biblical Literacy or Continuing Education Units (CEUs).

We hope each study group will consist of both casual and more intentional learners, and our design includes opportunities in class sessions for those engaging the material more deeply to share what they've learned with the others.

The Exploring the Bible Sponsors

The Benefactor

Exploring the Bible: The Dickinson Series is named in honor of its chief benefactor, Dr. Charles C. Dickinson III, a biblical scholar and long-time trustee of the Massachusetts Bible Society. Dr. Charles Dickinson was born in Charleston, West Virginia, on May 13, 1936; was educated there and at Phillips Academy, Andover, Massachusetts; and graduated cum laude in religion and philosophy from Dartmouth College, Hanover, New Hampshire. After serving three and a half years with the US Marine Corps in the USA and Far East, he studied theology and philosophy in Chicago, Pittsburgh, West and East Germany, at Yale University, and at Union Theological Seminary in New York. He received his B.D. (Bachelor of Divinity) and Ph.D. degrees in Pittsburgh in 1965 and 1973 respectively and did post-doctoral study at Oxford University and Harvard Divinity School. Dr. Dickinson has taught in Richmond, Virginia; Kinshasa, Zaire, Congo; Charleston, West Virginia; Rome, Italy; the People's Republic of China; Andover Newton Theological School; and Beacon Hill Seminars in Boston. He lives with his wife, JoAnne, and their son, John, in Boston.

The Author

This series was conceived and designed by Rev. Anne Robertson, executive director of the Massachusetts Bible Society, who also developed and wrote the three student texts and leader's guides. She is the author of three additional books: Blowing the Lid Off the

<u>God-Box: Opening Up to a Limitless Faith</u> (Morehouse, 2005); <u>God's Top 10: Blowing the Lid Off the Commandments</u> (Morehouse, 2006); and <u>God with Skin On: Finding God's Love in Human Relationships</u> (Morehouse, 2009). Rev. Robertson is an elder in the New England Conference of the United Methodist Church, is a winner of the Wilbur C. Ziegler Award for Excellence in Preaching, and is a sought-after speaker and workshop leader. She can be found on the web at www.annerobertson.org.

The Massachusetts Bible Society

Founded on July 6, 1809, the Massachusetts Bible Society is an ecumenical, Christian organization that has historically been a place where those across the theological spectrum of belief could unite for a common purpose. At the beginning of its history, that purpose was simply getting a copy of the Bible into the hands of anyone who wanted one, especially those without the means or opportunity to obtain one themselves. In more recent times, that work has been supplemented by the development of a variety of educational programs highlighting the importance of the Bible for faith, culture, history, and politics, as well as providing a forum for the many different voices of biblical interpretation. Exploring the Bible is a significant addition to those efforts and attempts to continue the historic tradition of being a place where those of many different faith traditions can unite for a common purpose—in this case, biblical literacy. You can find out more about the Massachusetts Bible Society at www.massbible.org.

You

<u>Exploring the Bible: The Dickinson Series</u> is made possible because you have elected to be a part of it. While we believe the course materials are

useful in and of themselves, it is the community of students and group leaders who bring those materials to life as you engage with one another in your classes and online forums. Just by participating, you are helping to raise the level of biblical literacy in our world. You can ensure that this ministry continues by completing the facilitator and student evaluations for each course, by purchasing the materials, and by telling others about Exploring the Bible: The Dickinson Series. There are also opportunities for you to provide scholarship assistance for future students, to attend training to become a group leader, or simply to offer moral or financial support to the mission of the Massachusetts Bible Society. Our most important sponsor is you. Find out how you can help at exploringthebible.org.

Our Theological Point of View

In the creation of this series there are several obvious biases:

- The Bible is a book that can and should be read by individuals both inside and outside the church.
- Understanding of the Bible is enhanced and deepened in conversation with others.
- The tools of scholarship are not incompatible with a faithful reading of Scripture.
- Diversity of opinion is both a welcome and a necessary part of any education—especially biblical education.

Beyond those points we have tried to give an unbiased theological perspective, describing differences of opinion and scholarship in neutral terms. Although named for and written by Christians, Exploring the Bible: The Dickinson Series is designed to be an educational tool, not an evangelistic tool. The Massachusetts Bible Society affirms that the making of Christian disciples is the job of the local church. These materials are designed either to fit into the overall disciple-making effort of a local church or into a secular environment where people of other faiths or of no faith can gain a deeper understanding of the nature and content of the Bible.

Course Administration

Obtaining Credit for Certification or CEUs

Those wishing to enroll in the certificate program or obtain CEUs for their work must fill out an application and do the work in an approved small-group setting. Those who simply work their way through the materials on their own are not eligible for credit or certification. To find out more or to obtain an application, go to exploringthebible.org/getting-credit.

You can find out all the details and download any necessary forms at exploringthebible.org/getting-credit.

Note that you must be a registered group leader with the Massachusetts Bible Society for any of your students to get credit. This is not difficult to obtain and is not necessary for leading an informal group. But you must register for any of your students to receive formal credit. You can find the application at exploringthebible.org/forms.

The Cost

Costs will vary depending on whether you are a casual student (which has no cost apart from the books) or are taking the course either for CEUs or certification (for which there is a fee). Please check our website at exploringthebible.org/getting-credit for more information, current rates, and information on discounts and scholarships.

Keeping in Touch

Go to exploringthebible.org to learn more or contact the Massachusetts Bible Society at 199 Herrick Road, Newton Centre, MA 02459 or dsadmin@massbible.org. You may also call us at 617-969-9404.

Note About Page References

The notation "LP" after a page number indicates the large print version of the Student Text.

Leading Exploring the Bible: The Dickinson Series

(Note: Some people contact the Massachusetts Bible Society in search of someone who would lead a group in their location. If you would be interested in such an opportunity, please contact us.)

Your Students

The Exploring the Bible student materials can be used by anyone, whether they're part of a formal class or not. It's designed, however, for a group of eight to fifteen adults to study together, and students will gain the most from the series if they participate in such a group. You may be part of a church or other organization that has recruited you to facilitate the class, or you may have just picked up the materials on your own and decided that you wanted to lead a group in your community. Either way, there are things to think about when putting a group together.

Who Would Be Interested in This Course?

There are three groups of people whose interest might be piqued by this series:

First are those for whom it is primarily designed: People who know little to nothing about the Bible and its contents. They don't know Adam from Abraham from Jesus and couldn't name a Bible story if you paid them. They might be Christians seeking knowledge of their own sacred text, members of another religion who want to learn about the Bible, or those of no particular faith at all who simply recognize the cultural, historical, and social impact of the Bible on world civilization. What they have in common is that, for all intents and purposes, they have never cracked open a Bible. Especially if they are Christians in a church, this group may be embarrassed to admit their degree of biblical illiteracy.

Second, there are many, many people who know a good bit about the contents of the Bible but next to nothing about the context of the Bible—for example, how it was put together and when, the history and culture of biblical times, and so on. This second group may also find a great benefit in Exploring the Bible: The Dickinson Series because of the inclusion of that type of information in the materials and exercises.

Third, there are (for want of a better term) Bible study "junkies." Found mostly (although not exclusively) in churches, these folks will sign up for anything at all with the Bible in the title on the off chance that there may still be some teensy bit of biblical information they're lacking.

Each of these groups can find some benefit in the study—no matter how much you already know about the Bible there is always more to learn, especially as you discuss passages with others. Problems may arise, however, when the various knowledge levels are grouped together, because the questions and issues that come up are qualitatively different for each type of group.

For example, groups two and three might start comparing this Bible text to another while group one is still trying to figure out who the characters in the story are. As the discussions move on without them, referencing stories and texts with which the first group is entirely unfamiliar, the first group starts to feel dumb and drops out, and you lose the very type of student the course is designed to help.

With some finesse and discussion control by the facilitator, the first two types of students can be mixed in the same class without too many difficulties (although ideally there would be one group of pure neophytes and a second group of those lacking only the contextual piece). The third group, however, really needs to be actively discouraged from taking the class as a student, unless the whole class has substantial knowledge. Otherwise they will almost certainly hinder learning in others.

I have seen this time and time again in groups designed for beginning Bible students. The junkies come, monopolize the discussions, and soon the real neophytes are dropping out with an apologetic, "Oh, I thought this was just for new people." Your Bible junkies should be encouraged to facilitate a class themselves or, if there are enough of them, a class could be made up of just this type of student. They also could be encouraged to simply read the materials on their own.

If the person absolutely cannot be dissuaded from attending (or if to do so will cause too much conflict), consider giving them some sort of title or special advisory role in the group—perhaps as a co-facilitator. This will at least keep other students from feeling embarrassed about their knowledge by comparison.

Getting the Right People Together

The key to having groups that are basically on the same level of Bible knowledge is both in your initial advertising and in your follow-up with those who express an interest. At the end of this guide on page 69 are some advertising blurbs you can use to announce the course and solicit interest. You can also, of course, write your own. To avoid the pitfalls of mixing incompatible Bible knowledge levels, it will be most helpful if your advertising asks people to contact you (or whoever is receiving the information) in order to "express interest" rather than "sign up." That gives you the opportunity for a follow-up conversation in which you can find out the person's relative level of biblical knowledge and make appropriate recommendations.

In gauging the level, don't give an impromptu Bible pop-quiz; just ask something along these lines: "We like to put together groups of people with similar levels of knowledge about the Bible. A lot of people—even in churches—really don't know the Bible at all, others know a number of the stories but don't really know how the Bible itself was put together or they may struggle in reading it. Still others have taken lots of Bible studies and are eager to know even more. Do you see yourself in any of those groups? Why are you interested in this course?"

A conversation like that allows you to let people know the parameters of whatever group is set up without sounding like you are giving anyone preferential treatment. Some possible responses to your callers' comments: "Gosh, Sarah, the only people who responded are those who don't even have a basic knowledge of the Sunday School stories. We have enough for that group but we didn't get enough for a group at your level of knowledge. We might even have enough for two of those basic groups. Would you possibly be interested in leading one?" Or, "Well, Zach, we have enough for a group, but most of them have a lot more experience with the Bible than you do. You're more than welcome to come to the class if you're comfortable with that—after all, the material was designed for those who haven't even cracked the book—or you can wait for another group. It's your call."

Ideally you should establish the dates and times for the class and begin advertising for students two to three months before the time of the first class, maybe more if you're part of a busy organization that schedules events six months to a year out. Give people enough time to get the dates on their calendars so that you can ensure the best attendance possible.

Advertise the course in places where the students you want to attract will see it. If you represent a church that wants to reach out into the community with this course, advertising only in the church bulletin or on the church website will not help you achieve your goal. And don't forget to mention the class on social media. If you are open to people outside of your church or community attending your class, go to exploringthebible.org to list your class for those who might be looking for a venue near them.

Opening Up to the Community

The Massachusetts Bible Society often hears from people who are looking for a Bible study course in their area. Because Exploring the Bible offers Continuing Education Units (CEUs) and a certificate program (for those who do the Extra Mile work in the Student Text), we would like to know if you'd be willing to accept student referrals from the Massachusetts Bible Society for your group.

If so, we'll be glad to post the details of your class on our website to let interested parties know where they can find a course and we will advertise your course to our e-mail list. To make this manageable for you, please be sure to set a registration deadline and send the information to us as soon as you know it.

We also receive occasional requests from churches or other organizations that would like to run a course but don't have a leader. If you would be willing to facilitate the course for others, please drop us a line and let us know.

Students Who Miss a Class

Class dates, times, and locations should be established far enough in advance that students can plan their schedules in a way that minimizes conflicts with other activities. From your initial contact with potential students onward, the importance of attending class, both for themselves and for others in the class, should be stressed.

Even so, scheduling conflicts will come up and students will miss classes from time to time. Those seeking CEUs or the full Certificate in Biblical Literacy may miss one class, if necessary. The homework from the missed session, however, still must be completed. Those informal students who would like a completion certificate for this one course may miss up to two classes.

If students are missing more than two sessions, they are missing at least half the course and it's worth asking them whether they would like to simply wait and take it at a time that's better for them. Every person who attends enhances the learning of others in the class. Those who miss classes are not just missing an opportunity for their own education but are hampering the ability of others to have the full group experience.

If a student wants to make up a class, that is solely up to you as the group leader. If you want to take the extra time, that's your call. It is not necessary.

It is helpful for you to have a backup leader, however, in case you have to miss a class for any reason.

Students Who Don't Do Homework

Your initial contact with potential students should include the information that there will be homework in the course—to a greater or lesser degree, depending on the level of recognition they are seeking. **The homework for informal students ranges from about twenty minutes to two and a half hours per week, depending on the session and the course. Extra Mile students can count on several hours each week.**

As with class attendance, the expectations are greater for those seeking CEUs or certification. Continuing Education Units and progress toward the full Certificate in Biblical Literacy will only be granted when all the regular and Extra Mile homework has been completed and not more than one class session has been missed. Completion certificates for informal students will only be granted when the facilitator verifies that the student has come to class prepared and has not missed more than two sessions.

You will, most likely, have at least a couple of students who simply don't complete the reading assignments, week after week. Sessions are designed so that even these students should be able to get something out of the class session. Be sure your students realize that it's better to come to class unprepared than not to come at all. They can still learn—they just won't have as rich an experience as they would otherwise.

If you notice that very few are able to complete the reading, you might consider holding sessions less frequently—perhaps every other week instead of every week, for example. Courses two and three have considerably more reading than course one, and if you have participants with busy lives they might appreciate a longer time frame. Of course if they are still just going to wait until the night before to try to cram it all in, having a longer stretch will not help.

Some reminders are built into the curriculum. The last element of every class session is a review of the homework for the coming week. You might also want to send an e-mail midweek to jog your students' memory—perhaps with a teaser from one of the questions for reflection in the Student Text. If someone has posted on the Exploring the Bible Facebook page, you could also send a brief e-mail notice inviting students to check out the new thread or new response.

Don't make a spectacle of or chide students who frequently are not prepared, especially in front of others. It's often helpful, however, to have a private conversation with such a student to see what the issues are that are preventing the work from being done. You might be able to offer some solutions or guidance. Remember the great caveat of Plato: "Be kind, for everyone is fighting a great battle." When your students finally meet God face to face, nobody is going to be asking them why they didn't do their Exploring the Bible homework. Keep perspective.

Dealing With Problem Personalities

One of the most difficult parts of leading any group, no matter what the topic, is the truly problem personality. While everyone can have a bad day and some people have quirks that can cause awkward moments, sometimes you'll run across participants who prevent the group from accomplishing its goals. They might consistently dominate the discussion and pull the group off track, make comments that are offensive and/or threatening, or exhibit other behaviors that either destroy the open and inclusive atmosphere or make getting through the material impossible.

If you should end up with "that guy" or "that gal" in your group and repeated attempts at (private) correction have not yielded a change in behavior, please talk either with your pastor or the Massachusetts Bible Society to resolve the issue. In rare cases a person might have to be asked to leave the group. And whatever you do, make sure you don't become "that guy" or "that gal"!

Your Class

Group Size

The session activities in this Leader's Guide assume a group size of eight to fifteen people. Sessions often call for the students to be divided into smaller groups for discussion. This both saves time and allows those who are reticent to speak up in a larger group to still have input and express their views.

This course will be challenging to do with fewer than eight students. Over the course of the study, someone will get sick, someone will suddenly be without transportation, someone's child will have a recital, someone will get called in to work, and you will find yourself trying to do a session with two students. Without a rich and varied discussion in class, students are not receiving the full benefit of the course, even if they are one of the two students who did show up. If you cannot recruit a class of at least eight students, consider rescheduling the course for another time or make sure you really have an attendance commitment from the ones you have.

If your church is small, consider reaching out to other churches in your area. These courses have been used successfully with both ecumenical and interfaith groups as well as groups that include atheists and agnostics. Think beyond the walls of your church or organization.

This course will be difficult to do with more than fifteen students. And fifteen is pushing it. This is a small-group study. With more than fifteen students it is easy to lose the intimacy that allows for the trust, bonding, and sharing that make small groups such a powerful learning environment. You will also be hard-pressed to keep within the session time frame of ninety minutes. If you have more than fifteen who are interested, consider dividing them into two classes.

If you have a large group and five or more are Extra Mile students (see p. v), you might also consider having one class of only those more intentional learners. Since they cannot receive the certificate or CEUs without full completion of the course (see p. ix), you are less likely to have attendance issues in that group.

As you progress beyond Course One in the series, you may have new students who have not taken the previous courses. This is especially true of the New Testament course, since many Christians tend to think the Old Testament is irrelevant and might skip the first courses to wait for the "real Bible." Our evaluations have shown that sometimes this has been a hurdle for the new students. The early courses give some important background both on the Bible itself and on the overall purpose and approach of the course. And, of course, a solid understanding of the Old Testament is critical for a proper understanding of the New.

While there is no need to forbid students to jump in to a later course if they haven't done the early ones, you should let them know that others who have done so have not gotten the same benefit as those who took the courses in order. You could also encourage such students to get the student books for the other courses to read in preparation.

Meeting Location

Your meeting space can either help or hinder the students' learning and will send unconscious messages about how open people should be about their thoughts and circumstances. While this is a class for which some students will receive various kinds of credit, a classroom atmosphere of students lined up in rows (or pews) in front of a teacher will not be ideal. Students should be in a setting where they can easily see one another as well as the facilitator, can engage in discussions (either in one group or in sub-groups), can enjoy refreshments without worry, and can sit for an hour and a half without discomfort.

Be sure to look for a space that can accommodate students with mobility issues or other types of disabilities. Remember that each course's Student Text is available in both regular and large print.

If you're leading a group in which everyone is familiar with one another and you're not accepting any referral students, then meeting in someone's home is ideal. If you're a church group, meeting in a home means you don't have to worry that six other groups want the church lounge the same night you want it, and the home atmosphere can make people feel…well…at home. Do be sure, however, that it is a home that, at least for that time, will be relatively free of distractions and that it can comfortably accommodate the number of people in your group.

If you want to draw in some new folks to your group, it's better to find a public location. This might be the aforementioned church lounge, a library or community center with available meeting space, or your local pub or coffee shop. As the group gets to know one another, you might decide to move elsewhere, but at the outset meet at a location that group members can easily find and get to.

Don't discount the possibility of hosting the class at another institution. Want students from the nearby college? Call the chaplain and see about getting space for the class on campus. Want to help seniors at the local assisted-living facility keep their minds active? See if you can use space right there. Does your congregation have an active prison outreach? Teach it there. A good host is always planning for the ease and comfort of the guests. Model biblical hospitality in your meeting space.

You Are a Facilitator

Many people feel intimidated by the thought of leading a Bible study. There is the perception that to lead people through a study of the Bible, one must be a learned biblical scholar or a pastor. That would be true if the course leader were developing the materials to be taught. With Exploring the Bible, however, the Massachusetts Bible Society has provided material that is grounded in solid biblical scholarship but that can be presented by those without specific biblical training. As a group leader, you are a facilitator, not a teacher. The information is in the books, you are just there to help people find their way through it.

Of course there's nothing wrong with having a biblical scholar or pastor lead this course. It is simply our belief that such qualification is not necessary to effectively introduce students to the Bible. You can do this!

But I Don't Know The Answers!

Undoubtedly there will be class sessions in which questions arise that aren't addressed in the Student Text or Leader's Guide. When that happens and you don't know the answer, don't panic. You're not in this alone. Let's review your options for dealing with questions that stump you. Whatever option you choose, please be sure to record the question.

If the same question keeps popping up in different groups, we'll know we should address it in a revision of the Student Text.

- If the question is specific to a particular Bible passage, ask students to look in the notes associated with that passage in their study Bibles. Ask: "Does anyone have notes that address the question?" This approach helps students familiarize themselves with how a study Bible can help them.

- If your meeting location has wi-fi access or a tech-savvy student has a smart phone, type the question into Google and see what comes up. This can help students see how to research their own questions when they arise outside a class setting. There are new Bible study tools appearing online all the time. You can find a listing of some we find helpful at www.massbible.org/how-to-study-bible.

- Suggest that someone submit the question to the Ask-a-Prof service of the Massachusetts Bible Society. This is a free service and can be found at www.massbible.org/ask-a-prof.

- Encourage students to "like" the Exploring the Bible Facebook page to discuss their questions with students in other groups and the Massachusetts Bible Society staff.

- Volunteer to research the question yourself and bring back a response the next week. In doing that research, you can ask other members of your church, check the Internet or library, or contact the Massachusetts Bible Society for a response.

- Remind students that not all questions have "answers" per se. Sometimes a variety of opinions will be the best you can do. Be sure students know that Appendix 4 on page 99 (p. 127 LP) in their Student Text suggests resources for finding answers to their questions.

Atmosphere Is Everything

Learning is more than absorbing a set of facts. To truly learn and grow, students must feel that their honest questions are taken seriously and that they won't be judged for expressing their opinions. Perhaps the most important role of the group leader is ensuring that the class environment is "safe" in that regard. Students are willing to take risks in learning when they feel a class environment is safe.

This course was not created as a tool for Christian evangelism and faith formation, although the Massachusetts Bible Society is certainly not opposed to such activities. With Exploring the Bible, however, we wanted to create a vehicle in which people of all faiths or no faith could learn more about the Bible for any and all reasons. We believe that faith formation is the role of the local church. What we have provided in Exploring the Bible is an educational tool that can be used to anchor that faith formation in local churches and to provide information about the Bible that can be accepted in secular and interfaith settings.

To make that possible, the class setting and atmosphere must work to embrace not only very, very basic questions (for example, "Is 'Christ' Jesus' last name?") with respect, but must also be open to those who might challenge traditional Christian interpretations or express dislike for biblical passages. Even if you have an entire group of professing Christians, there are probably beliefs and opinions in the room that contradict Christian orthodoxy or run afoul of the doctrines of a particular tradition or denomination. As long as the question is sincere and isn't coming from a problem personality purposely trying to stir the pot, your job is to make sure that the person asking feels heard and respected and that the question is given a fair hearing.

How the first such question is handled will determine the extent of real learning that can occur. Being able to hear challenging questions and comments without bristling is a much more important qualification for being a leader of these courses than Bible knowledge. Of course any statements that demean another race, gender, sexual orientation, or anything else should be swiftly corrected and apologized for.

Should the Leader Participate?

In most cases, the person leading the class should not participate as a class member in the exercises, even if you are learning the material along with the students. Any one of the exercises during class sessions could easily take up the entire class time. You're needed as a timekeeper and cannot fulfill that role as effectively if you're involved in discussion yourself. You should, however, be completely familiar with the exercise that the class is doing and with the material on which it's based. A thorough checklist for class preparation is provided at the beginning of each session's lesson plan.

You're also in a role of authority, even if you don't feel particularly authoritative. For some students, when the leader weighs in on a subject (especially when that leader is also a pastor or other respected person in the community), it can come across as pressure to conform to that leader's opinion. When that occurs, learning is stunted, since it may be perceived that not all opinions or positions can be freely considered.

That's not to say you must always remain silent and aloof. There may be an occasion when you need to participate for reasons of group cohesion. If, for example, a class has a member with a difficult personality who is making discussion in smaller groups difficult, you might volunteer to be that person's partner for one of the exercises. You should also step in to help de-escalate any conflicts, to protect those expressing unpopular opinions, to prod a stalled discussion, or to get a discussion back on track.

If group members are asking for your opinion, try to dissuade them or at least give your opinion last so that others don't feel constrained from expressing different thoughts. And even then, tread with caution. The authority figure speaking last can seem to negate or even mock all different responses that have been given prior. If you must weigh in, do so last and with a huge dose of humility and respect for other opinions expressed. When you can affirm any part of what someone else thinks, do so.

The only time more intentional participation might be warranted is if you end up with a group that is thinking rigidly and as a monolith. If there are no divergent opinions in the group, something is amiss either in class atmosphere or in student imagination. There are always differences of opinion among human beings, even if the people are part of the same faith tradition or even the same church.

If those alternative opinions are not being expressed, it's part of your job to break down whatever walls are keeping them out. That might involve you throwing out some different ideas for discussion, even if they're not opinions that you favor. Just keep your disfavor to yourself and encourage a discussion of the ideas on their own merits. That will help students to see that the expression of different opinions is not only safe but also encouraged and will help them learn to think outside the box.

Please Give Us Feedback

Near the back of this guide are course evaluations for both students and group leaders. Every Student Text has that same course evaluation in it and you can find it online at exploringthebible.org/forms. It is so helpful to us to receive these evaluations. The lesson plan for Session 6 includes time for evaluation and provides instructions for returning evaluations to us. Because these courses are being published in a print-on-demand format, we can make adjustments to the text very easily.

Whether you are letting us know about a typo that we missed or letting us know the ways that the course did or didn't work for you and your group, your feedback helps us to make this material the best it can be. We read every single evaluation that comes to us and while we love to hear praise and sometimes use those statements for testimonials, we truly want to know if something about the course material or presentation has been problematic. If the same criticisms keep coming across the desk, we fix the problem.

Please let us hear from you. It really helps.

Becoming a Registered Group Leader

If you just have informal students in your group, then there is no need to register with the Massachusetts Bible Society. If you have Extra Mile students who are seeking credit, however, they can only get that credit with a registered group leader. It isn't hard to register, but it is necessary for anyone in your group to get formal credit for their work.

To register, go to exploringthebible.org/forms and you will find two documents. One is the actual Application to Lead Groups for Credit and the other is the document that spells out the details of working with students seeking credit. The latter document is under "Other Documents of Interest" on the Forms page and is called "Expactations and Requirements for Leading a Group for Credit." Read that and send us the application.

If you have any questions, feel free to call or e-mail us.

Overview of Class Session Elements

Check-In

Beginning in Session 2, each class session begins with a set of two check-in questions about the material to be dealt with in that session:

- What is one thing I have learned from this material?
- What is one question I have related to this week's topic?

These questions are posed in the Student Text to help participants prepare for the next class, so ideally they have already thought about them. **These are not designed to be discussion questions. Responses should be one or two sentences at most, simply stated by students without any elaboration.** It's simply a way to gauge where students are and to allow participants to hear, in their classmates' responses, questions or issues they may not have thought about themselves. It is also a helpful tool to get people focused on the material at hand and to remember some of the themes and stories they read about.

One way to assure that check-in time doesn't turn into a full-blown discussion is to simply record the responses on your white board or newsprint or on paper. That way, questions won't get lost in the shuffle and if there isn't a sufficient response during the rest of the class session it can be carried over or addressed through one of the means discussed in the "But I Don't Know the Answers" section on page xxiii. **This technique of writing questions to be answered later is often called the "Parking Lot"—a place to park your questions and issues for a bit to see if they're answered by later activity.**

Bible Activity

Most sessions contain a thirty-minute activity that examines a particular biblical passage or story in detail. The goal of this activity is to become more familiar with a well-known Bible story or passage and to get some practice thinking critically about the text. Students will be divided into two or more groups and encouraged to use the resources in their study Bibles as well as the text itself.

For some students, this program will represent an entirely new way of looking at the Bible and could be unsettling at times, depending on their background. Go gently in such instances and respect the struggles some might have in, for example, finding that the creation stories in Genesis 1 and Genesis 2–3 don't match. Don't rush to find solutions, but don't dismiss student concerns, either. You may want to ask some students to formulate their concerns into questions or issues that can be put in the Parking Lot to see if further light is shed along the way.

The Bible Activity is usually wrapped up with groups reporting back in some way about what they've discovered in their study of the text.

Life Connection Activity

Most sessions also contain a thirty-minute activity on a second well-known passage of the Bible. The difference is that in this activity the questions are more reflective. Here the objective is to explore the ways in which the Bible has relevance in daily life—either in the individual life of the student or in the broader scope of community and culture.

When students are asked to reflect more personally about a Bible passage, the groups are typically smaller (two to three people) so that it's a bit easier to open up to someone else. These responses are typically not conveyed to the group at large but are left in the sharing of the small groups.

In both the Bible and Life Connection Activities, students will learn more if they're with different groups each week. Encourage students to group with those they haven't before and recommend that couples and close friends split up into different pairs or groupings for these exercises. If there is great reluctance to do this, it need not be forced, but do keep trying for new group permutations.

Review of Homework

The Student Text contains homework—one assignment for all students and a second assignment for those seeking certification or CEUs. The latter are referred to as the Extra Mile students, and in order to earn their certification, they must complete **both** sets of homework. At the end of each session, spend about five minutes looking over the homework for the next session to resolve any questions and to offer a constant reminder that there is homework to be done.

Extra Mile Presentations

To be sure that those who have chosen to engage in more in-depth study of the material don't feel they're simply jumping through hoops for their certification, several of the sessions include a fifteen-minute period for those who have done this extra work to present what they've learned. Depending on the number of Extra Mile students in your group, this will require some judgment calls on your part to keep to the time frame.

Not every session includes an Extra Mile presentation. When the Extra Mile work has been personal and reflective, sharing of these assignments has not been included so that students might feel freer in their expression. The presentations are suggested, however, when the homework has included extra research on a topic related to the subject of the particular session.

Please make private notes about these presentations that briefly answer the following questions:

- **Who made a presentation?**
- **Did the presentation reflect that the assignment had been done?**
- **Any other notes you believe would be helpful in judging whether the student has done the appropriate level of work for the extra recognition they are to receive.**

While the Extra Mile work is required for certification and CEUs, others are welcome to do these exercises if they wish. If they do, they should be encouraged to share their findings along with the others. Be sure to keep the same set of notes for these students as well, just in case they decide at some point during the course to go for the certificate or CEUs.

At the conclusion of the course, these private notes should be submitted to the Massachusetts Bible Society to help with student evaluation. Most of the Extra Mile assignments include some written work. Students should keep these in a folder and submit them to the Massachusetts Bible Society at the conclusion of the course.

If you have a group (or a particular session) with no Extra Mile students, give the extra time to one or more of the other session activities.

First and Last Sessions

The first session of each course includes elements to help the group begin to get to know each other and lay the groundwork for future class sessions. There is some kind of icebreaker, a review of the nature and scope of the series, and guidelines for establishing a Bible study covenant.

It is always helpful if students can get books ahead of the first class and begin reading, but there are many reasons why that might not be possible. The exercises in the first session always assume that students have not read the first session of the Student Text. These exercises will have students actively using their student books more than in later sessions, where they will use the Bible more than their Student Texts.

The last session of each course is also a bit different. There is time in these lesson plans for both oral and written evaluation, celebration of the students' achievement, presentation of certificates, and housekeeping issues. The exercises in these sessions often reflect back on the course as a whole.

There are two kinds of certificates for each course. Informal students get a Certificate of Participation. These are available at exploringthebible.org/forms for you to download, fill out, and give directly to your students.

Extra Mile students get a Certificate of Completion. These must be requested from the Massachusetts Bible Society. You are prompted to send the information to us at the conclusion of session four so that there will be time to process these certificates and get them to you for the final session.

Lesson Plan

ORIENTATION TO THE BIBLE 1

Objectives

- To find out more about one another
- To share learning goals and explain course process
- To work with several elements in the Session 1 Student Text

Materials Needed

- Nametags and markers
- Bibles for students who don't bring one
- Student Text for each student if these have not been procured ahead of time
- Newsprint and stand or whiteboard with discussion questions written out
- Markers (for the appropriate surface)
- Two or three different study Bibles
- Simple refreshments, if appropriate to the setting, are always a nice touch at every session, but especially at the first and last.

Handouts

- I Heard It in the Bible (you will need one for each student); see page 79
- Class Contact Information form (you will need one to circulate among class members); see page 77

Leader Preparation

- Read the "To the Student" portion of the Student Text along with the material in the Student Text for Session 1.
- Do the homework for Session 1.
- Read the introductory materials in this Leader's Guide.
- Become familiar with the texts and activities for the Session 1 class session.
- Write out the Icebreaker questions and the discussion questions for the Life Connection Activity on the newsprint/whiteboard for easy reference.
- Find and prepare needed materials.

Gathering

The initial class announcement should invite students to come ten to fifteen minutes before the actual start of the ninety-minute session. During this time, each student should receive a nametag and their Student Text (if not procured ahead of time). It is always a nice gesture to have simple refreshments available. Make sure students add their contact information to the Class Contact list, and be sure to determine which, if any, of the students will be doing the class for certification or CEUs.

Make sure students are aware of the following regarding their contact information:

- During the course the information will be used by the group leader to contact students about course matters.
- Unless otherwise indicated, contact information will be shared with the Massachusetts Bible Society at the end of the course.
- The Massachusetts Bible Society will not share that information with any third party.
- Students will then receive one e-mail from the Massachusetts Bible Society to determine how much and what kind of contact a student would like to receive going forward. These options might include:
  - *Being a part of the regular Massachusetts Bible Society mailing list*
  - *Receiving information related to future Exploring the Bible courses, conferences, or activities*
  - *Receiving all event notifications from the Massachusetts Bible Society*

Session I Activities

Welcome (5 Min)

Refer students to pages xiii-xx (xxi-xxiv LP) in the Student Text and quickly highlight the following:

- This is **just the first of three courses** in Exploring the Bible: The Dickinson Series.

- "Most of the arguments and conflicts over the Bible aren't really about what the Bible says but about **how to interpret what it says**." (Student Text p. xiii, p. xv LP) Be respectful in your disagreements.

- **Questions** are the key to this study. Become an explorer/investigator.

- **Pick your level of engagement**—informal student or Extra Mile/certificate student.

- **Keep a journal** in which to record your personal reflections.

- During class time **we will only discuss a portion of what is in the Student Text**. To get the full benefit of the material, you must **do the homework**.

Icebreaker (7 Min)

Ask students to pair off with someone they don't know or don't know well.

Invite each student to briefly interview the person with whom he/she is paired, seeking answers to the following questions. (Have the questions written on newsprint/whiteboard so that students can refer to them during their interviews.)

Notes

LESSON PLAN I: ORIENTATION TO THE BIBLE

Session 1 Activities

Notes

- What is your partner's name? What is the correct pronunciation? Does your partner have a preferred nickname?
- Where does your partner live? How long have they been in that community?
- On a scale from 1–10 (with 1 being low and 10 being high), how familiar is your partner with the contents of the Bible?

Allow one to two minutes for each interview.

After the time has elapsed, ask each student to introduce his/her partner by answering the three questions. (Prompting from partners is allowed.)

Introduction and Guidelines for Class Discussion (15 Min)

Introduce yourself to the class if there are any participants who are unfamiliar to you. Explain your own background in the study of the Bible. If you're a pastor or have a degree in a biblical field, say so. If not, don't apologize. Explain that you're there as a facilitator of well-prepared material and that you'll often be learning along with the class.

Inform students that when questions arise for which you have no response without additional time and/or research, you will put them in the "Parking Lot" (see Leader's Guide p. xxx) to address at a later stage.

Remind students that they may also go to the Exploring the Bible Facebook page to post their questions or discuss class material with other Exploring the Bible students.

Session 1 Activities

Be sure that students are aware of these important points about <u>Exploring the Bible: The Dickinson Series</u>:

- This course is one of three that allow students to receive a Certificate in Biblical Literacy or Continuing Education Units from the Massachusetts Bible Society. Students seeking certification or CEUs will have additional assignments that need not be completed by those who are only taking the course informally.

- Starting with the second session, those doing the extra work will have an opportunity each week to share the additional information they've learned with the rest of the group.

- At any time during these six sessions, a student may switch into or out of the certificate or CEU program. Those who switch into the more formal program partway through must go back and complete the earlier Extra Mile assignments.

- Call attention to the sections on pages vi-vii of the Student Text about the series benefactor, Charles Dickinson, writer Anne Robertson, and the Massachusetts Bible Society to be sure they are aware of who is behind the series.

Direct students either to the description of the series at the beginning of the Student Text (p. iii, p. iv LP) or to exploringthebible.org for more information.

Ask students to turn to the Covenant for Bible Study on page 98 (p. 126 LP) of the Student Text (p. 76 of this guide).

Notes

Session 1 Activities

Notes

- Read the six principles aloud with a different student reading each one.
- Ask whether everyone is comfortable with this covenant and willing to commit to it.
- See if there are questions or suggested additions.

Ask: "Is there anything else we should practice to help make this a productive learning environment for all?"

If not already raised by students, raise the question of the use of technology and social media during and after class sessions. For example:

- How will your group deal with cell phones?
- Are you open to having someone using Twitter to describe the class sessions to their followers?
- What about posting comments about class on social networking sites like Facebook?

Write any suggestions on the newsprint/whiteboard and ask if students are willing to make these a part of their covenant. If there are things the group agrees to add, ask each student to write them on the these blank lines.

Session 1 Activities

Life Connection Activity: Vanessa's Story (25 Min)

Objective: *By reading about a fictional person, students gain a point of entry for discussion of their own previous experiences with the Bible.*

Part 1 *(5 min)*

- Ask students to turn to the beginning of Session 1 (page 2).
- Have students take turns reading a paragraph of Vanessa's story aloud. Just go around the room, with each student taking the next paragraph until the story is completed. Participants who are uncomfortable reading aloud should be permitted simply to say "pass" at their turn and the next person can continue the story. *(Note: This method of reading a text should be used whenever possible in class activities.)*

Vanessa's Story

The billboard was huge and Vanessa had no trouble reading it in the slow highway traffic. "Judgment Day is coming on May 21. The Bible is never wrong. Be prepared." Vanessa chuckled to herself. "Couldn't the world end now?" she wondered. "This traffic is making me crazy."

But still she thought about it. Vanessa didn't really know much about the Bible. Her family had not been churchgoers, although they always had called themselves Christians. But Sundays were typically filled with other things and before she knew it, Vanessa was grown

Notes

Session 1 Activities

Notes

Vanessa's Story Cont.

and married and continuing life in much the same way. Jesus seemed like a decent guy, and she taught her kids to share, to be polite, and to avoid the "bad crowd." Wasn't that the essence of it? Honestly, she didn't know.

The Bible had been in her face a lot this week, especially from her son. Jeremy had begun to show a real interest in art and just yesterday she had taken him to the city museum.

"Mom, what's happening in that painting?" he had asked, time and time again.

Her answer was always the same. "It's a Bible story, honey."

"But what's happening?" Jeremy persisted.

Vanessa was embarrassed that she had no more information to give him. She wasn't even really sure they were Bible stories, but that's what she said when she saw someone in the painting with a halo.

And then there had been the letter from her representative in Congress. It asked for her support and claimed that the government had strayed far from the principles of the Bible and the faith of our founding fathers. Well, she couldn't say for sure whether that was true or not. Was she being asked to vote for a godly man or a religious fanatic? She had no way of knowing.

Before she knew what she was doing, Vanessa had left the traffic jam behind and taken the exit for the mall. "I need to just get a Bible and read it," she thought. "This is silly. I think

Session 1 Activities

Vanessa's Story Cont.

I'm well educated, but I don't know even basic answers to things that affect my son's education or my ability to vote wisely. And should I be preparing for that meeting on May 22? Could the world really be coming to an end?" Soon the large brick façade of the bookstore loomed.

When Vanessa finally found the section of Bibles, she discovered that it made the traffic jam seem preferable. There were tons of the things—all different. First were all sorts of different English translations, although some were called "paraphrases." What was that about? There were Bibles for those in recovery, for women, for children, for those interested in archaeology. There were "study" Bibles and "devotional" Bibles. Some had highlights in red, some highlighted different things in green, and still others had different verses in purple. There was the Poverty and Justice Bible, the Amplified Bible, the New Spirit-Filled Life Bible. To top it all off, some Bibles included books that other Bibles didn't. Her eyes began to blur. She left empty-handed.

Notes

Session 1 Activities

Notes

Part II *(10 min)*

When the story is complete, invite students to pair up and discuss the following questions. (The questions appear in the Student Text at the end of the story on page 3 and should already be written out on the newsprint/whiteboard as part of your class preparation):

- What obstacles have you encountered in trying to read the Bible?
- What brings you to this study now?
- What do you hope to gain when you have finished?
- When and how did you discover that there was such a thing as a Bible?
- Was that a positive or negative experience?

Part III *(10 min)*

- Ask students to rejoin the larger group.
- Ask pairs to comment on the kinds of obstacles to reading the Bible that group members reported.

Session I Activities

Bible Activity: I Heard It in the Bible (30 Min)

Objective: To highlight the presence of the Bible in our language, stressing the importance of biblical literacy for cultural engagement.

Part I *(18 min)*

- Give students the **I Heard It in the Bible** handout on page 79 of this guide and ask them to turn to page 4 (p. 5 LP) in their Student Text.

- Review the boxed paragraph about Bible referencing on page 4 (p. 5 LP) in the Student Text and be sure the method is understood.

- Review the instructions for the I Heard It in the Bible exercise on p. 4 (p. 5 LP) of the Student Text.

- Divide the students into groups of two or three and ask them to do the exercise in their groups **without** looking at the answer key.

Bible Referencing

The earliest biblical scrolls don't separate passages into chapters and verses as contemporary Bibles do. Those aids were added in the Middle Ages.

The traditional way to reference a passage in the Bible is by citing first the book, and then the chapter number followed by a colon and the verse number(s). So, for example, the command to "love your neighbor as yourself" is found in the book of Leviticus, chapter 19, verse 18. It is notated as Leviticus 19:18.

Notes

Session 1 Activities

Notes

Part II *(7 min)*

- When their answers have been recorded on the handouts, ask everyone to turn to the answer key on page 9 (p. 12 LP) in the Student Text to see how they did.

- Explain that this activity shows students how the Bible has become an integral part of Western culture and note that there are many other passages that could have been used.

Answer Key For "I Heard It In The Bible"

1. Drop in the bucket
2. Salt of the earth
3. Forbidden fruit
4. Armageddon
5. Fly in the ointment
6. A house divided against itself cannot stand
7. The blind leading the blind
8. As old as the hills
9. By the skin of your teeth
10. Fight the good fight
11. Go the extra mile

Session 1 Activities

Part III *(5 min)*

Comment on items 2, 3, and 4 under the "Why All the Problems?" section of the Student Text (p. 4-5, p. 4-7 LP). Note that the Bible:

- Pervades our language, art, music, and architecture
- Plays a role in politics
- Can be hard to understand
- Has many interpreters, making it hard to know which sources to trust, thus the benefit of studying with a trusted community

> **2. The Bible is everywhere.** Biblical allusions can be found throughout our language, literature, art, music, and architecture—it's difficult to claim a cultural education without at least a passing knowledge of the basic stories and texts of the Bible.
>
> Rembrandt created over three hundred works of art on biblical themes. If your children enjoyed <u>The Chronicles of Narnia</u>, they enjoyed an allegorical interpretation of Christ's passion. Literary works by Tolstoy, Dickens, Flannery O'Connor, Dante, Milton, Steinbeck, Shakespeare, and a host of others are rife with biblical references. There are hospitals and charitable organizations across the country and around the globe that take their name from Jesus' parable of the Good Samaritan.
>
> As a case in point, try out the following exercise to see how the Bible permeates the English language.

Notes

Session 1 Activities

Notes

I Heard It in the Bible: Look up the following passages (your Bible should have a table of contents to help you find the books) and see if you can determine what common English phrase or idiom comes from that passage. Answers can be found at the end of this session.

Note: For those using a pre-2010 edition of the New American Bible, the Ecclesiastes reference above is found in Ecclesiastes 9:18 instead of Ecclesiastes 10:1.

3. The Bible plays a role in politics. Biblical claims, for good or for ill, also play a role in American political life, and many of the histories of nations described in the Bible are still being played out in the geopolitics of the world today. The complexities of Middle East conflicts are deeply interwoven with biblical texts. There's a whole lot that can't be understood about our world without at least some familiarity with the Bible, whether you see it as a sacred text or just another book. Its influence on history, culture, and contemporary society is too large to ignore. Of course those who do claim the Bible as the sacred text of their faith need to dig in for the sake of their own spiritual growth.

A July 2011 Gallup poll found that three in ten Americans believe that the Bible should be interpreted literally, and some political leader is being named as the Antichrist almost as frequently as someone is predicting the end of the world based on biblical prophecy. The Bible crops up wherever you go.

4. The Bible can be hard to understand. For a long time the complexities of

Session 1 Activities

the Bible and the difficulties of getting books into people's hands put the complete burden of conveying its contents on the church and clergy. Gutenberg's printing press, Bible translators, and changing sensibilities have altered all that. You can now get a Bible in your own language, access all sorts of study guides and information, and shape your own faith accordingly. In fact, there is now so much information available at the click of a mouse that it can be hard to know what sources to trust. That is one of many reasons to do serious Bible study in a community setting.

REVIEW of the homework assignment (given at the end of Session 1, on page 9 (p. 12 LP) in the Student Text) for the next session (8 min):

Note that the Extra Mile work for this week will not be shared in Session 2. There is no Extra Mile presentation in Session 2. This is indicated in the student homework section below.

- Articulate again that those seeking certification or CEUs need to do the Extra Mile assignment in addition to the regular homework. Others are welcome to do the Extra Mile if they choose but it's not required for those taking the class informally.

- Alert students to the fact that they will be asked to share information about the study Bible they have selected as part of the next class session and that a major portion of class time will be exercises using their new Bibles. **Bottom line: They should do the homework and get a study Bible before the next class session.**

Notes

LESSON PLAN 1: ORIENTATION TO THE BIBLE   15

Session 1 Activities

Notes

Keep a folder for each of your Extra Mile students, placing in the folder all their written work and any of your notes about their work. Be sure to submit this material to the Massachusetts Bible Society immediately upon the completion of the course so as not to delay their certification or CEUs.

Homework (All Students)

- ☐ Read through Session 1 material and study the sections on "The Bible and the Fabric of Life" (p. 5-7, p. 7-9 LP) and "Choosing a Bible" (p. 7-8, p. 9-11 LP).

- ☐ Read through Session 2 material in the Student Text and respond in writing to the two questions at the end of Session 2 on page 23 (p. 29 LP) in preparation for class check-in.

- ☐ Select and obtain the study Bible you will use for the remainder of this course.

Extra Mile (CEU and Certificate Students)

- ☐ Read the section in Session 1 called "The Role of Your Brain" (p. 6-7, p. 8-9 LP).

- ☐ Using the reflection questions at the end of that section as a guide, write an essay of approximately five hundred words on the issues of trust and skepticism raised by the Bible. This is a reflective rather than an academic essay and you will not be asked to share it during Session 2. What are the issues for you?

Lesson Plan

CHOOSING A BIBLE 2

Objectives

- To begin to familiarize students with the helpful tools of their study Bibles
- To expose students to some well-known biblical texts and stories
- To help students discover differences in scholarly opinion about the biblical texts and to think about helpful ways to approach those differences

Materials Needed

- Nametags
- Bibles as needed
- Newsprint and stand or whiteboard with discussion questions written out
- Markers (for the appropriate surface)
- Several study Bibles in different translations and with different perspectives
- Maps for the Bible GPS exercise, just in case students have selected study Bibles that do not have the needed information. A map showing Tarshish can be difficult to find in a study Bible. One can be found online at www.bibleatlas.org/full/tarshish.htm and you can either look at this online in class or print it out to show students if their study Bibles do not go this far west.
- Parking Lot list

Handouts

- Stumbling Blocks handout on page 81 of the Leader's Guide

Lesson Plan

Leader Preparation

- Read the material in the Student Text for Session 2.
- Do the homework for Session 2.
- Select two or three study Bibles that use different translations. (This allows you to interject some alternative interpretations or additional information in the event that everyone in your group comes back with the same study Bible and/or translation.)
- Become familiar with the texts and activities for the Session 2 class session.
- Research any questions that came out of Session 1 for which you promised a response.
- Write out Check-in questions on newsprint or whiteboard. (You can save doing this each week if you write on something that can be saved and brought back to each session.)
- Write out Bible references for Famous Verses and Author! Author! exercises on newsprint/whiteboard.
- Print out map of Tarshish (or have the link ready to show through an Internet connection) in case it is not available in the study Bibles selected by students.
- Do the Author! Author! exercise on page 21 of this guide with the several different study Bibles you are bringing. Make sure there is at least one with a differing opinion of authorship or date in case the Bibles brought by students are all in agreement.
- Find and prepare needed materials.

Session 2 Activities

Check-In (10 Min)

From this session on, begin each class meeting with a ten-minute check-in. Each session should include the following (brief) responses from each person:

- What is one thing that was new to me in this material?
- What is one question that this week's topic raises for me?

This is not the time to discuss what they learned or to try to answer their questions. It's simply a way to note student observations and to spur the thinking of others.

- Remind students of the value of questions and an inquiring mind.

Bible Activity: Show and Tell (45 Min)

Objective: To help students become more familiar with the tools and helps available in their study Bibles and to gain some experience using them.

- Go around the room and have students briefly tell their classmates what study Bible they've selected for the course.
- Once all have shared, explain that they'll have a chance to practice using it with the following exercises:

Notes

Session 2 Activities

Notes

Part 1: Famous Verses *(13 min)*

- Give one of the following verses to each student, making sure that all the verses are given out (with a small group, some individual students may get more than one; with a larger group, some students may get the same verse).

- Have each student find their passage in their Bibles. Encourage them to use their table of contents or other indices to find the book if they do not know where it is.

- When they've located it, have each student read the verse aloud. Explain that these are all verses that those who want to be biblically literate should know. As they read their passage aloud, each person should recite the chapter and verse as well as naming their translation. For example, "I'm reading John 3:16 from the New Revised Standard Version."

John 3:16	Proverbs 1:7
Isaiah 40:31	Leviticus 19:18
Philippians 4:13	1 Corinthians 13:13
Exodus 3:13–14	Deuteronomy 6:5
Matthew 6:24	

Session 2 Activities

Part II: Author! Author! *(13 min)*

- Explain that study Bibles generally have introductions to each book of the Bible with some background on how, when, and where the book was put together.

- Ask students to get into groups of twos or threes and assign to each group one of the following books.

- Each group should look up their book in their Bibles and find the translator's introductions.

Amos	1 Corinthians
Mark	Revelation
Genesis	

- Give groups a few minutes to skim the intro to look for the following information:
  - *Who wrote this book of the Bible?*
  - *When was this book of the Bible written?*

- Have the groups report what they found out about each book. Ideally, there will be at least a couple of different study Bibles in the room with differing information. *If the Bibles brought by students agree in every instance, bring out information in one of the several study Bibles you have brought.* (You should find differences of opinion on Mark, Genesis, and Revelation at least.) Don't try to resolve differences or allow a discussion about them. Simply have groups find and report what they've learned.

- Stress that the purpose of this exercise is to allow students to see what kind of information a study Bible can provide and to realize that even good scholars sometimes disagree.

Notes

Session 2 Activities

Notes

Part III: Bible GPS *(13 min)*

Most study Bibles include maps of the biblical world at various stages of history.

- Have students find the book of Jonah and read the first three verses silently. While reading, each student should jot down the names of the three places mentioned in those verses. When finished, they should have listed Nineveh, Tarshish, and Joppa.

- Once all have identified the three place names, ask students to divide into groups of twos or threes (or whatever configurations are necessary to be sure that each group has at least one person with maps in his or her study Bible). Then ask each group to try to locate those three places on at least one of the maps. Offer extra kudos to anyone who can name the modern countries that contain those ancient locations.

Answer Key

1. Nineveh is in Iraq
2. Tarshish is on the coast of Spain
3. Joppa is in Israel

Note: *The location of Tarshish is disputed, as there are other possible locations in southeastern Turkey and India or perhaps cities by that name in all three locations.*

Part IV: Discussion/Response/Questions *(6 min)*

Session 2 Activities

Life Connection Activity: Stumbling Blocks (30 Min)

Objective: *To help students think about a Bible passage in light of contemporary situations and to begin to sort out their own thoughts about the relevance of the biblical texts to daily life.*

Part I *(5 min)*

- Ask students to find Romans 14 in their Bibles.
- Taking turns, have students read the entire chapter aloud.

Since they may be using different translations, have students read a certain number of verses each rather than relying on paragraphs, which may differ from one translation to another.

This passage was in their homework assignment but some may not have read it.

Part II *(25 min)*

- Give each student a copy of the handout titled, "Stumbling Blocks." Have them work individually with the questions, making notes of their thoughts on the handout. (6 min)
- Divide the class into groups of four or five and have each group discuss the questions. (13 min)
    - *What do you think is the main point Paul is making in this chapter?*
    - *Paul is specifically addressing differences about early Christian behavior that arose from the culture of the first century C.E.. Do you think his words would help or hinder people in conflict over what translation of the Bible should be used?*

Notes

Session 2 Activities

Notes

- *Can you think of other conflicts among people in our own day and age that could be helped by Paul's advice to the Romans?*
- *Are there limitations to his advice or places you believe it would not be helpful?*
- Bring the groups together and ask for responses to the question, "What is the key element you take away from this discussion?" (6 min)

REVIEW the following homework assignment for Session 3. Students will find the assignment on page 23 (p. 30 LP) of the Student Text. (5 min)

- Point out that Sessions 3 and 4 have a lot more readings from the Bible than other sessions and they should plan their homework time accordingly.

Session 2 Activities

Homework (All Students)

- ☐ Read the text for Session 3, along with each of the Bible readings listed.

- ☐ Think about the questions associated with each reading.

Extra Mile (CEU and Certificate Students)

- ☐ Pick one of the books of the Old Testament and research the question of its authorship and the time and circumstances of writing.

- ☐ Prepare an essay of five hundred to seven hundred words about what you discovered. Your study Bible should have information about these issues in an introduction to each book. Begin there, but also do research online or look in the introductions to other study Bibles to see if there are differences of opinion. There almost always are. What is the evidence used to determine the answers?

Notes

Lesson Plan

OVERVIEW OF THE OLD TESTAMENT 3

Objectives

- To become familiar with two well-known Old Testament stories
- To begin to learn how to look critically at a text
- To think about how a Bible text might offer life lessons and insight

Materials Needed

- Nametags
- Bibles
- Newsprint and stand or whiteboard to compile story notes
- Markers (for the appropriate surface)
- Sheet with Check-in questions
- Several study Bibles in different translations
- Parking Lot list
- Optional: Small, smooth stones—one for each group member (see note at the end of the Life Connection Activity on page 31)

Leader Preparation

- Read the material in the Student Text for Session 3.
- Do the homework for Session 3.
- Become familiar with the texts and activities for the Session 3 class session.
- If the differences in the creation stories in Genesis are new to you, do a bit of extra research to become familiar with the topic. Wikipedia's entry on "Genesis Creation Narrative" has a good overview of the scholarship.
- Determine whether you have any students doing the Extra Mile work (and, if so, how many there are) and plan the session timing accordingly. See the note with the Extra Mile presentation on page 30).
- Write out the discussion questions for the Bible and Life Connection Activities on newsprint/whiteboard.
- Research any questions that came out of Session 2 for which you promised a response.
- Find and prepare needed materials.

Session 3 Activities

Notes

Check-In (10 min)

Allow each participant to respond briefly to the following:

- What is one thing that was new to me in this material?
- What is one question that this week's topic raises for me?

Bible Activity: In the Beginning (30 min)

Objectives: *To familiarize students with a famous portion of the biblical text. To help students see the complexity of the creation narratives and, by extension, the Bible as a whole.*

Part I (15 min)

Divide the class into two groups of roughly equal size.

Assign one group Genesis 1:1–2:3 and the other group Genesis 2:4–25. Instruct them to read their section aloud in their group (taking turns reading around the group) to look for and make note of the following (which should be posted on the newsprint/whiteboard for reference):

- The order in which things were created
- The literary genre in which the account is written **Note: Some may need the explanation that a genre is a category of literature like poetry, history, parable, letter, etc.**
- Reasons provided in the text for various aspects of creation
- The means by which God created

WHAT IS THE BIBLE?

Session 3 Activities

• Anything else group members feel is noteworthy

Ask each group to assign a note taker and reporter to share their findings with the other group.

Part II *(15 min)*

Bring the groups back together to share their findings.

• What did they discover?

• What differences did they observe?

Ask all students to check their study Bibles for notes that might address the differences.

Use the following questions, which appear in the Student Text on page 30 (p. 40 LP), for discussion:

• What important truths do these stories teach?

• Would those truths change if the accounts were not factual?

• Have you encountered these stories outside of church?

• What do you like about them?

• What questions do they raise for you?

Extra Mile Presentations *(15 Min)*

Those working toward CEUs or certification should have written an essay about the date and authorship of an Old Testament book of their choosing. Others may have done this voluntarily. Allow those members of your class (if any) to share their findings. Each person will have more or less time depending on how many in the class have completed this assignment.

Notes

Session 3 Activities

Notes

If you have more than one or two **Extra Mile students, there will not be time for all of them to present.** In that case, select one or two for this presentation and then choose different students for Extra Mile presentations in other class sessions.

If there are no Extra Mile students in your group, you can use this time to:

- Deal with Parking Lot questions/issues.
- Expand the discussion time for one or both of the class activities.
- Randomly select a book of the Old Testament and ask students to examine the introduction to that book in their study Bibles, looking for information about authorship. Allow students to share findings.
- Allow students to give feedback on how the course is going for them now that they are halfway through.

Life Connection Activity: A Boy and a Giant (30 Min)

Objective: *To become familiar with a famous story from the Bible and to help students see that biblical stories often have themes that resonate with contemporary life.*

Part 1 *(10 min)*

Ask participants to open their Bibles to the story of David and Goliath in 1 Samuel 17.

Session 3 Activities

Have students recap the story for one another in case some have not read it. (If you have a lively group, you might even have them do an impromptu role-play of the story.)

Part II *(20 min)*

When all the story basics have been brought out, divide the class into groups of twos or threes to respond to the following questions (which should be written out on the newsprint/whiteboard):

- Were there surprises for you in reading this story?

- Aside from purely factual material, do you think there is any "truth" to be learned from this story?

- Have you ever been in a conflict in which you felt like the little guy/gal facing a giant—where the odds seemed stacked against you? How did you respond?

- Have you ever been the giant who was challenged by someone without your level of power and resources? How did you respond?

- Do you think the story of David and Goliath might have resonance outside of faith communities? In what way?

A nice touch is to give each student a smooth stone at the conclusion of this exercise as a reminder of what they have shared, but finding the stones might be an issue. Aside from stones you might find in certain areas outside, smooth stones are often used in home décor in vases and small indoor fountains. Stores with home accent or décor sections will often have small bags of such stones that are perfect for this exercise.

Notes

Session 3 Activities

Notes

REVIEW of the following homework assignment for Session 4. (5 min) Students will find it on page 39 (p. 53 LP) in the Student Text.

- Again, remind students that there is a lot of Bible reading in Session 4 and they should be wary of leaving all the homework until the last minute.

Homework (All Students)

☐ Read the text for Session 4, along with each of the Bible readings listed.

☐ Think about the questions associated with each reading.

Extra Mile (CEU and Certificate Students)

☐ Research the letters known as the Pastoral Epistles (1 and 2 Timothy and Titus) and prepare a five-hundred-word written report contrasting the arguments both for and against Paul's authorship of these letters.

Lesson Plan

OVERVIEW OF THE NEW TESTAMENT 4

Objectives

- To become familiar with two important New Testament narratives
- To begin to distinguish the differences in the Gospel accounts
- To think about the ways the Bible can teach life lessons and other "truth" through fictional stories

Materials Needed

- Nametags
- Bibles
- Newsprint and stand or whiteboard to compile story notes
- Markers (for the appropriate surface)
- Sheet with Check-in questions
- Several study Bibles in different translations
- Christmas cards with nativity scenes, a crèche, or other artwork depicting the Nativity. See the instructions in Part I of the Merry Christmas exercise on page 35.
- Parking Lot list

Lesson Plan

Leader Preparation

- Read the material in the Student Text for Session 4.

- Do the homework for Session 4.

- Become familiar with the texts and activities for the Session 4 class session.

- If the differences in the Gospels relative to the Christmas stories are new to you, do a bit of extra research to become familiar with the topic. You can read an overview on Wikipedia in the entry for the "Nativity of Jesus."

- Determine how many students are doing the Extra Mile work and plan the session timing accordingly.

- If you think your class might be averse to the drawing exercise, gather some Christmas cards or other artwork with nativity scenes to use as examples. A crèche also serves the purpose nicely.

- Write out the discussion questions for the Bible and Life Connection Activities on newsprint/whiteboard.

- Research any questions that came out of Session 3 for which you promised a response.

- **Prepare a list for the Massachusetts Bible Society of all students who you anticipate will complete the course as Extra Mile students, making sure all names are spelled correctly.**

- **Send the list of names to dsadmin@massbible.org and indicate the postal address where certificates should be sent.**

- **Note that the Certificate of Participation you will give to informal students is available for you to download and print yourself at exploringthebible.org/forms. You only need to request the Certificate of Completion for Extra Mile students from MBS.**

- Find and prepare needed materials.

Session 4 Activities

Check-In (10 min)

Allow each participant to respond briefly to the following:

- What is one thing that was new to me in this material?
- What is one question that this week's topic raises for me?

Bible Activity: Merry Christmas (30 min)

Objectives: To become familiar with one of the central narratives of the New Testament. To allow students to discover that there are differences between the Gospel accounts.

Part 1 (5 min)

Ask for a volunteer to draw/depict a typical nativity scene on the board or newsprint.

- Solicit help from the group about what should go in the scene as the volunteer draws.

If your group is either averse to or unable to do the drawing, you can also use any of the following:

- Show (either on a laptop or by bringing in an image) a famous painting depicting the nativity. A quick Internet search on "famous nativity paintings" will bring up many for you to choose from. You can download them to a laptop and show them on the screen or print them out and pass them around the class. Ask students to settle on one that they believe is representative.

- Use a crèche and ask students to manipulate the pieces to form a representative scene.

Notes

LESSON PLAN 4: OVERVIEW OF THE NEW TESTAMENT   35

Session 4 Activities

Notes

- Examine Christmas cards with various elements of the narrative. Ask students to settle on the one that they believe is representative.

Part II *(15 min)*

Divide the class in half.

Have individuals in the first group read Matthew 1:18–2:12 silently to themselves; individuals in the other group should do the same for Luke 1:26–38 and 2:1–20. As they read, individuals should make notes on the following (which should be written out before class on the newsprint/whiteboard for easy reference):

- The events in the narrative
- The people who are named in the account
- The places referred to in the story

Once everyone in the group has finished reading and making notes, individuals should share with their group what they have discovered.

Each group should then determine how they would alter the original nativity representation (from the drawing, crèche, painting, cards, etc.) to reflect the account they have just read and assign a reporter to share their new rendering with the entire class.

Session 4 Activities

Part III *(10 min)*

Bring the two groups back together and ask each reporter to share their new nativity scene.

Explain to the group that Mark does not include a Christmas narrative and that John has only the more mystical introduction of Jesus to the world in John 1:1–14 (which was part of the Student Text reading for Session 4).

Ask for comments/reactions related to the way in which we generally see what took place.

Extra Mile Presentations *(15 Min)*

Students doing the Extra Mile homework were asked to research the debate surrounding the authorship of the Pastoral Epistles in the New Testament. Others may have done this voluntarily. Allow those members of your class (if any) to share their findings. Each person will have more or less time depending on how many in the class have completed this assignment.

If you have more than one or two Extra Mile students, there will not be time for all of them to present. In that case, select one or two for this presentation and then choose different students for Extra Mile presentations in other class sessions.

If there are no Extra Mile students in your group, you can use this time to:

- Deal with Parking Lot questions/issues.
- Expand the discussion time for one or both of the class activities.

Notes

LESSON PLAN 4: OVERVIEW OF THE NEW TESTAMENT

Session 4 Activities

Notes

- Make your own presentation on the debate concerning authorship of the Pastoral Epistles. The Wikipedia entry for "Pastoral Epistles" gives a relatively balanced overview of the various positions.

- Allow students to give feedback on how the course is going for them now that they are halfway through.

Life Connection Activity: Family Values (30 Min)

Objectives: To familiarize students with one of the best known of Jesus' parables and to experience the way ancient parables can resonate in contemporary situations.

Part I (10 min)

Ask participants to open their Bibles to the parable of the Prodigal Son in Luke 15:11–32.

Have students recap the story for one another in case some have not read it. If you have a lively group, you might even have them do an impromptu role-play of the story.

Part II (20 min)

When all the story basics have been brought out, divide the class into groups of twos or threes to respond to the following questions:

- Were there any surprises for you in this reading?

- What truth(s) do you think Jesus was trying to convey with this parable?

- Think about the three main characters in the story: the prodigal, the elder brother, and the

Session 4 Activities

father. Do you know any of these characters from your own observation or experience?

- What would be the benefits or drawbacks of using this story to guide parents of rebellious children?

- Does this story connect with your own life (either past or present) in any way? How does it speak to your current life situation?

REVIEW of the following homework assignment for Session 5. It can be found on page 53 (p. 71 LP) of the Student Text. (5 min)

Homework (All Students)

☐ Re-read the section titled "A Word About 'Truth'" from Session 3 (p. 28, p. 71 LP).

☐ Read the text for Session 5, along with each of the Bible readings listed.

☐ Think about the questions associated with each Bible reading.

☐ Think about the questions under "Your Own Beliefs" on page 65 (p. 86 LP).

Extra Mile (CEU and Certificate Students)

☐ Look at the questions for reflection with the Jonah reading on page 62 (p. 82 LP) and, in five hundred to seven hundred words, write a response.

☐ Be prepared to lead a discussion of those questions during Session 5.

Notes

Lesson Plan

THE BIBLE AND ITS AUTHORITY 5

Objectives
- To become familiar with two well-known Bible passages
- To recognize the various ways that people interpret biblical texts and to try to understand their positions
- To start each student pondering where their thinking falls on the various continuums

Materials Needed
- Nametags
- Bibles
- Newsprint and stand or whiteboard to compile story notes
- Sheet with Check-in questions
- Markers (for the appropriate surface)
- Several study Bibles in different translations
- A snack of goldfish crackers is a fun way to recognize the Jonah story
- Parking Lot list

Leader Preparation
- Read the material in the Student Text for Session 5.
- Do the homework for Session 5.
- Become familiar with the texts and activities for the Session 5 class session.
- Determine whether you have any students doing the Extra Mile work and plan the session timing accordingly.
- Based on your knowledge of the particular members of your group thus far, determine whether the Life Connection Activity will be a role-play or a discussion.
- Write out the discussion questions for the class activities on newsprint/whiteboard for easy reference.
- Research any questions that came out of Session 4 for which you promised a response.
- Find and prepare needed materials.

Session 5 Activities

Notes

Check-In (10 min)

Allow each participant to respond briefly to the following:

- What is one thing that was new to me in this material?
- What is one question that this week's topic raises for me?

Bible Activity: A Big Fish Story (22 Min)

Objectives: To become familiar with a famous story from the Bible and to think about the relationship between truth and fact.

Note the shorter time frame for this activity.

Part I (10 min)

As they did with the story of David and Goliath, have the group recap the story of Jonah, which they should have read along with the material for Session 5.

List the main events of the narrative on the board or on newsprint as they are mentioned.

When the important elements have been recounted, ask each individual to write down a ranking for the book of Jonah on a scale of 1–10 with 1 being complete fiction and 10 being factual in every detail.

Session 5 Activities

Part II *(12 min)*

Divide the class into small groups of twos and threes to discuss the following questions:

- What score did you give the book of Jonah. Why?
- What truth(s) do you find in this story?
- Would the truth(s) you just identified change in any way if the genre of the story turned out to be a parable rather than history? Why or why not?

Extra Mile Presentations (15 Min)

The Extra Mile students were asked to write their responses to the discussion questions on page 59 (p. 82 LP) of the Student Text.

Select one of the Extra Mile students to lead the rest of the group in a discussion of the questions below.

If there are no Extra Mile students in the group, you should lead the discussion.

- Think of a fable/story you have heard that was fiction but conveyed an important truth. What was true and not true in that fable/story?
- What does it mean for something to be true?
- What is the difference between facts and truth?
- What do you think it means to say the Bible is true?

Notes

Session 5 Activities

Notes

Life Connection Activity: Household Rules *(38 Min)*

Objectives: To become familiar with a well-known section of the Pastoral Epistles and to experience the different ways that this type of text can be interpreted.

Part 1 *(10 min)*

- Ask students to turn to 1 Timothy and read 2:8–3:13 aloud, taking turns reading around the room (and then to keep their Bibles open to that passage).

- Ask students to count off from one to four to form four groups. As the facilitator, you should not take a number.

- Have everyone turn to the descriptions of the absolute positions on pages 57-61 (p. 75-81 LP) in the Student Text.

- Identify groups as #1: Sole Author, #2: Human Work, #3: Rulebook, #4: Ancient Relic.

- Have each group think about and discuss how those in the absolute position they have been assigned might respond to the passage from Timothy.

- Explain that this may or may not represent their own position—the purpose of the exercise is to try to see the text through a variety of lenses.

Session 5 Activities

The Absolutes

What Role Did God Play in the Creation of the Bible?

The two absolute poles related to this question are:

- God as the **sole author**, dictating the Bible word for word to human beings who were protected by God from introducing any error of any sort into the text. For the purposes of discussion, we'll call this the "Sole Author" position.

- The Bible as a completely **human work**, subject to both human bias and error, in which God played no role at all beyond being the subject about which people wrote. We will refer to this position as "Human Work."

Now let's look at these two absolute positions in more detail.

Sole Author

Those who see the Bible as devoid of any error of any type (a position often referred to as "inerrancy") tend to arrive at that conclusion because they believe God had a direct hand in crafting every moment of human history, including the writing and preservation of the writings that became our Bible. In this view, there is only one biblical author, and that is God. Those who put pen to paper had such a direct connection to the Divine that they became incapable of conveying any sort of error—religious, scientific, historical, social, or any other kind. God spoke and the writers wrote it down, just as God intended it. If God said that 10,000 men marched into battle, then that's how many there were. Not 10,001 and not 9,999—there were 10,000.

This view has God speaking in every verse for all time. There is no historical context that would make the text require interpretation, no personal bias of the author or the author's community that would slip in. No part of the Bible truly contradicts any other—it is all the same truth of God—and if there should be seeming contradictions, it just highlights our need for more information. The plain meaning of the text is there for all to see. It is what it is and it says what it says, and that's that. The Bible is completely and totally inerrant, even (for some) in translation.

Session 5 Activities

The Absolutes *Cont.*

In this group are what have been dubbed the "young-earth creationists," who believe that the days of creation in Genesis 1 refer to twenty-four-hour time periods and, when combined with the number of generations listed in the genealogies, calculate that the earth is a mere six thousand years old.

Human Work

We learned in science class that for every action there is an equal and opposite reaction, so what lies at the opposite end of this spectrum about God's role is no surprise. For this group, God had no part at all in the creation of the books that became our Bible. It is, in their eyes, a purely human creation and God didn't provide so much as a cup of coffee for those who labored over its pages.

Of course atheists would fall into this view of the Bible by definition, since they don't believe there is a God to create, inspire, or even offer editorial suggestions. But there are also people of faith who have simply decided that working in and through human authors in any way is simply not how God operates.

This position does not necessarily imply that the Bible has no authority or relevance, however. Remember that while these questions have overlap, they are distinct questions. Many in this category recognize the impact of the Bible on culture and the arts or find the teachings of Jesus or the calls to justice made by the prophets to be worthy of consideration and even emulation. They simply believe that the source of such relevance and authority is solely human and therefore prone to errors, contradictions, primitive moral structures, and political self-justification.

What Authority Does the Bible Have in Daily Life?

The two absolute poles related to this question are:

The Bible is a **rulebook** that should be consulted and has a solution for every problem and circumstance in both private and public life. We will refer to this pole as "The Rulebook."

Session 5 Activities

The **Absolutes** Cont.

The Bible is an **ancient relic** that has no contemporary application or authority. This position we will call the "Ancient Relic."

Now let's examine them in more detail.

The Rulebook

This group is composed of those who believe that the answer to every single question in life can be found somewhere in the Bible. It's a rulebook that trumps every law of every nation or organization. Those who believe in God as Sole Author often overlap with this group at least to some extent. After all, if you think God dictated all the biblical laws and there is no chance that they contain any human error, bias, or historical limitation—well, you'd be hard-pressed not to follow them to the letter.

There is also a tendency here to see every passage in the Bible as indicative of some kind of law or rule. Certainly there are laws aplenty, as we saw in Session 3. But this group will generally go beyond the explicit laws and see biblical narratives, Psalms, and other genres of literature in the Bible as containing at least hints and clues to the rules by which God wants us to live. An example of that would be in referencing the poetry of Psalm 139:13b, "You knit me together in my mother's womb" as guidance for the issue of abortion.

The Rulebook position, however, faces a question that those in the Sole Author camp do not. What do you do with things the Bible doesn't mention? Some believe that if the Bible doesn't specifically forbid something, it is permissible. Others believe all that is allowed are those things specifically permitted in the pages of the Bible.

An example of the latter can be found in the area of music in the Church of Christ denomination. The Church of Christ does not allow for instrumental music, but does include the singing of hymns in their worship. Two things are at play here. The first is that they see only the New Testament as an authoritative rulebook. That eliminates all the harps and lyres, tambourines and trumpets of the Old Testament. The second is their belief that if the New Testament doesn't mention a given practice, it is forbidden. After the Last Supper, Jesus and his disciples are

Session 5 Activities

The Absolutes

recorded as having sung a hymn before they left. That allows for singing. However, there are no musical instruments mentioned in New Testament worship, so they are excluded.

Ancient Relic

Those who hold this absolute position might look at the Bible and say "ancient relic" with the love and curiosity of the archaeologist or with the disdain of someone who despises all it stands for. Either way, they share a belief that whatever the Bible is, it is not to be used as an authority either in private or public life and has nothing helpful to say to contemporary ears.

As with the Sole Author and Rulebook positions, there is often overlap between those who view the Bible as a solely human work and those who believe it is an ancient relic, but there are distinctions to be made. Just as those who see the Bible as a human work would allow for some human works (including laws) to have authority and relevance, so those who see the Bible as an ancient relic might still hold out for some role that God could play.

There are those who view the Bible as containing divine inspiration of some kind but for a different era in time or for a different group of people. There are those who believe it has authority for those who choose to accept it, but not for themselves. Still others believe that God is always doing something new and that the old is, therefore, to be discarded or only viewed as a relic of a past faith, even if the originals came from the very mouth of God.

Session 5 Activities

Part II *(7 min)*

Once participants are clear on the position they represent, ask them to prepare for a debate/discussion in which they will adopt their absolute position on whether/how the instructions in the Timothy passage should be applied in daily life, both inside and outside the church.

Ask for one group to begin the discussion and for others to state their positions and respond.

Use the following questions to prod the debate:

- Should the instructions be enforced only in the church or should they be the law of the land?
- Are some instructions more important than others?
- Are there general principles that can be gleaned even if a particular instruction is disregarded?
- Are there historical or cultural circumstances to be considered?

Part III *(10 min)*

Indicate a timeout and ask students to turn to and review the descriptions of the more moderate positions on pages 62-64 (p. 82-85 LP) of the Student Text.

Ask groups 1 and 2 to moderate their positions using the language of inspiration and groups 3 and 4 to moderate their positions using the language of general principles.

Resume the discussion with these more moderate positions and revisit the questions from Part III to prod the debate.

Notes

Session 5 Activities

The Moderates

Of course most people, including most Christians, do not find themselves in any of those absolute categories, although each of us probably leans toward some of them and away from others.

For example, one of the things I learned in doing ecumenical work was that Catholics and Protestants use the word "inerrant" differently. When Protestants claim an "inerrant" view, they usually mean that the Bible contains no errors of any type, as we discussed in the previous section. It is an absolute position. When Catholics use the term, however, they mean to say that the books of the Bible are without error **in the matters that God was intending to address**.

With the Catholic view, you have some room for scientific and historical inaccuracies and contradictions, because God was not thought to be writing a textbook for those subjects. God is conveying religious, moral, and spiritual truth in the Bible and it is those matters and those alone that remain above error. In fact, the Pontifical Biblical Commission in 1993 stated that, "fundamentalism [by which they mean the Protestant view of inerrancy] actually invites people to a kind of intellectual suicide."[2]

Once you leave the absolute positions on our two questions about God's role and the Bible's authority, each question tends to have a term that defines the long sliding scale between the poles. For the question about God's role in the creation of the Bible, that word is "inspiration."

Inspiration

Those who speak of the Bible as "inspired" believe that human beings definitely wrote the Bible (i.e., it was not strict dictation from God), and those human authors might have included their own agendas, biases, and factual inaccuracies. The language of inspiration makes room for biblical contradiction and errors, both in the original writings and in translation. Of course the assumed degree of those errors and biases

---

[2] Pontifical Biblical Commission, "The Interpretation of the Bible in the Church" (document prepared for Pope John Paul II, presented March 18, 1994, with preface by Cardinal Joseph Ratzinger). Available online at catholic-resources.org/ChurchDocs/PBC_Interp.htm.

Session 5 Activities

The Moderates Cont.

would determine whether a person was closer to the Sole Author absolute or the Human Work at the other end of the spectrum.

For those who speak of inspiration as it relates to the Bible, God is present and active in its creation, but not solely responsible for its contents. In some indefinable way, God "inspired" the biblical writers to record events, stories, poetry, teaching, and all the rest to show us what faithfulness has looked like in a variety of times and places. From that, we can take what is applicable to our own lives and create our own version of faithfulness.

When people use the word "inspired" about the Bible, they mean that it is more than just any old book. It is sacred—perhaps in a way that can't quite be defined, but sacred nonetheless. God is saying something in its pages—or at least in some of the pages.

Principles

When it comes to our second question, "What authority does the Bible have in daily life?" the term that dominates the sliding scale is "principles." Where the absolutes see hard and fast rules that should be applied literally and in the same way across time and space, those elsewhere along the line talk more of guiding principles and moral examples.

People here begin to look at many biblical specifics as being bound to the time or culture in which they were written but still see in them a general moral code that should have authority for contemporary life.

For example, take the law from Deuteronomy 25:4, which reads, "Do not muzzle an ox while it is treading out the grain." For the absolute position, this means nothing if you don't have an ox. It is about muzzling an ox and only an ox and only if it is treading grain. If your ox is treading grapes or if your donkey is treading grain, you can muzzle away. With an absolute rendering of the law, most Americans can turn the page and move on.

But for those who believe that it is acceptable to adapt the text to new situations or who want to extract general principles of ethics, there are

Session 5 Activities

The Moderates Cont.

all sorts of opportunities that flow along a continuum. Some might only move to include other animals that tread grain. Some go further into the realm of principle and apply the law to address broader concerns of animal welfare, humane farming, or even human labor laws.

Again, for most people it is not all or nothing. Most people will grant you that faithfulness to the Ten Commandments (at least those relating to social interaction) is a good idea and good for society, even if many of the other biblical laws are cast into the fog of cultural irrelevance.

On the flip side, even those who claim absolute literal inerrancy in all matters are seldom seen stoning people, as is commanded in a number of biblical verses for a variety of crimes from adultery (Leviticus 20:10) to sassing your parents (Leviticus 20:9, Deuteronomy 21:18-21). Few are those who refuse to mix wool and linen in the same garment (Leviticus 19:19), at least on biblical grounds. We tend to mix it up in our rules as well as our garments. The trick is removing our own self-interest from the equation so that we don't end up enforcing only laws that benefit us and turning the ones we don't happen to like into more general principles.

Session 5 Activities

Part VI *(8 min)*

Bring the discussion to a close and debrief with the following questions:

- Did arguing for a particular position make you more or less likely to consider the merits of that position—or did it have no effect?

- During the course of this exercise, what helped move the discussion forward or make it productive?

- In the same way, what hindered the discussion or made it difficult?

- Has your own position on the authority of the Bible moved as a result of this exercise?

REVIEW of the following homework assignment for next session, which is found on page 66 (p. 88 LP) of the Student Text (5 min):

Notes

Session 5 Activities

Notes

Homework (All Students)

- ☐ Read the text for Session 6.
- ☐ Select one of the ten archaeological topics described and search for additional information you can find out about the work being done in that area.
- ☐ Be prepared to share three to five additional bits of information about your selected topic at the final group session, but recognize that if your group is large, not everyone will have a chance to present.

Extra Mile (CEU and Certificate Students)

- ☐ Do the same homework assignment, but choose three topics instead of just one.
- ☐ Write out the additional information you have gleaned about each of the three topics but select only one for your class presentation.

Lesson Plan

ARCHAEOLOGY AND THE BIBLE 6

Objectives

- To learn how the science of archaeology informs the study of the Bible
- To glean feedback on the course material and experience
- To identify questions or issues that need follow-up
- To celebrate the achievements of the students in completing the course

Materials Needed

- Nametags
- Bibles
- Newsprint/whiteboard
- Markers (for the appropriate surface)
- Sheet with Check-in questions
- Certificates of Participation for all informal students and Certificates of Completion for Extra Mile students. The latter are obtained from the Massachusetts Bible Society and the former are available for you to download and print at exploringthebible.org/forms (See Leader Preparation for Session 4.)
- Parking Lot list
- Refreshments

Handouts

- Student Evaluation (one for each student) on p. 65 of this guide
- #10 blank envelope (one for each student)

Lesson Plan

Leader Preparation

- For this last session, consider whether your group would enjoy sharing a meal together. If there has been a bonding experience during the course for students, it would be entirely appropriate to extend the final session time to include a meal in someone's home, at a church, at a restaurant, or at some other location appropriate to the means and situation of your group. At the very least, there should be some sort of refreshments served.

- Download and print Certificates of Participation for What Is the Bible? from exploringthebible.org/forms. Prepare a certificate for every informal student to hand out at this session.

- You should have already requested Certificates of Completion from the Massachusetts Bible Society for any of your Extra Mile students. (See instructions for Session 4.)

- Read the material in the Student Text for Session 6.

- Do the homework for Session 6.

- Become familiar with the texts and activities for the Session 6 class session.

- Read through the instructions on page 62 of this guide for conducting the evaluation and providing the Massachusetts Bible Society with the final class documentation.

- Research any questions that came out of Session 5 for which you promised a response.

- Find and prepare needed materials.

Session 6 Activities

Important things to note about this session:

The structure is different from that of other sessions, with the bulk of the session devoted to sharing the research students have done.

Keep a watch on the clock during the Research Activity so that the wrap-up at the end is not shortchanged. Limit the number of presentations if needed.

Check-In (10 min)

Allow each participant to respond briefly to the following:

- What is one thing that was new to me in this material?
- What is one question that this week's topic raises for me?

Notes

Session 6 Activities

Notes

Research Activity (60 min)

Objectives: To help students become aware of the grounding of the biblical narratives in particular places and times and the way that grounding is connected to historical research.

The homework at the end of Session 5 asked each student to do some further research on one of the ten archaeological topics described in Session 6. Extra Mile students were asked to research three topics.

Invite people who want to share their findings to do so and then invite others who also researched that topic (or who might know something further about it) to chime in with their findings. *(If Extra Mile students have not done the work, this should be noted with the student in private as it will have to be completed before certification can be issued.)*

Guidelines for sharing research:

- What I did
- Where I went
- What I found
- What questions remain

If it turns out that no one has done any research, chances are they have not read the text either. In this event, return to the Student Text, pick a topic, and have students read the material about it in the Student Text aloud. Ask how many have heard of the topic before this class and get their reactions. Do as many as you have time for. If you have Internet access in your meeting location, you might also assign students to do some research on the spot.

Session 6 Activities

The more common problem is too many presentations. This is generally a popular session and it is easy for students to get wrapped up in the research they have done. If you have a lot of students and they have all selected different topics, you may have to use your discretion and limit the number of presentations. Those who have selected the same topic should present together.

Note that Extra Mile students were asked to research three topics but were told to select only one for presentation and other students were told in the homework assignment that they might not get to present.

The ten topics presented for research in the Student Text are:

- Where is the Garden of Eden?
- The Flood and Noah's Ark
- Were There Hebrew Slaves in Egypt?
- Mt. Sinai, The Ten Commandments, and the Ark of the Covenant
- The Temple Mount in Jerusalem
- The Walls of Jericho
- The Dead Sea Scrolls
- The Life of Jesus
- The Shroud of Turin
- Other Finds Related to the New Testament

Notes

Session 6 Activities

Notes

Wrap-Up (10 min)

Remind students of the "Help! I Have Questions!" section on page 99 (p. 127 LP) in their Student Text (Appendix 4) to resolve any questions that remain unanswered for them from the course material or to help with new questions that may arise from continued study.

Help! I Have Questions!

- If the question is specific to a particular Bible passage, look in the notes associated with that passage in your study Bible. Are there notes that address the question?

- Does someone else in your group have a different study Bible? Does it have any helpful notes?

- Google is your friend. It is quite likely that if you type your question into an Internet search engine verbatim, you will come up with more "answers" than you thought possible. Ditto for just putting in a Bible verse reference. These results, however, are unfiltered and will range from well-informed responses to the conclusions of the truly unbalanced or the simply ignorant. It is sometimes difficult to tell the difference if you don't have a biblical education yourself, so approach this option with caution. It will, however, give you a sense of the range of ideas out there.

- Submit the question to the Ask-a-Prof service of the Massachusetts Bible Society. This is a free service that takes your question to thirty-five professors from seminaries

Session 6 Activities

> ### Help! I Have Questions!
>
> and universities across the US and the UK. Participating professors come from a variety of denominations and faith traditions and represent both liberal and conservative viewpoints. You can read more about them and ask your question at massbible.org/ask-a-prof.
>
> - "Like" the Exploring the Bible page on Facebook to discuss your questions with students in other groups and the Massachusetts Bible Society staff.
>
> - Ask your group leader or another religious leader you trust for help.
>
> - Remember that not all questions have "answers" per se. Sometimes a variety of opinions will be the best you can do.

This is a time to get oral feedback about the full course. The written evaluation is done in the next section.

Appoint someone (maybe yourself) to take detailed notes about the responses to better inform your facilitator's evaluation.

Ask the following questions:

- What were your expectations of this course and were those expectations met?

- Did you enjoy the class activities? What was appealing about them? What wasn't appealing?

- Do you know more about the Bible now than you did when you started? How did this class contribute to this?

Session 6 Activities

Notes

- Did this course make you more (or less) interested in delving more deeply into Bible study?
- Was there anything you learned about the Bible that really surprised you?
- Did you feel that the course was unbiased in its approach to the text?
- Is there additional feedback you would like the Massachusetts Bible Society to hear?

Evaluation and Celebration (10 Min)

- Collect any outstanding homework from Extra Mile students and remind them of the last homework assignment for this lesson on page 86 (p. 115 LP) of the Student Text (and listed below).

- Congratulate all students and hand out their certificates one by one. Recognize the hard work they have put into the course and sing their praises. Celebrate the accomplishment of your students!

- Hand out the student evaluations and envelopes. Students should fill out the evaluations at this session and seal them in the envelope before turning them back in to you.

- Before letting students go, remind them that this is just the first of three, six-week courses in <u>Exploring the Bible: The Dickinson Series</u>. Refer them to the "There's More I Want to Know!" section on page 87 (p. 116 LP) of their Student Text.

Session 6 Activities

Extra Mile (CEU and Certificate Students)

☐ Prepare a final essay of five hundred to seven hundred words describing your experience with the course and its contents. Have your views of the Bible changed? If so, in what way(s)? Were your views of the Bible confirmed? In what way(s)? What unanswered questions about the Bible are most important to you now?

☐ Submit this essay to your facilitator or to the Massachusetts Bible Society along with any other outstanding materials needed for your certification.

Once the Final Session Is Complete

Mail or scan and e-mail the following back to the Massachusetts Bible Society:

- Student Evaluations
- Your Facilitator Evaluation
- Homework from your Extra Mile students
- Your notes about the performance of the Extra Mile students
- Your class contact list

Mailing address: 199 Herrick Rd., Newton Centre, MA 02459

E-mail: dsadmin@massbible.org

Please return this evaluation to:
Massachusetts Bible Society, 199 Herrick Rd.,
Newton Centre, MA 02459
or e-mail to dsadmin@massbible.org.

STUDENT EVALUATION

Course (circle one):   I   II   III

Why did you take this course? Were your expectations met?

Did you do this study with a group or on your own?   ☐ Group   ☐ Alone

Did you take this course for certification or CEUs?   ☐ Yes   ☐ No
If yes, please be sure that all of your written work is submitted to the Massachusetts Bible Society by either yourself or your group leader at the conclusion of the course.

Did your group have a mix of "Extra Mile" and informal students?   ☐ Yes   ☐ No

    If "yes," did you find the mix helpful?   ☐ Yes   ☐ No

Why or why not?

STUDENT EVALUATION

Who was your group leader? _____

Scale: 1 - most negative, 10 - most positive

Please rate your leader on the following using a scale of 1-10.

- _____ Creating a welcoming and inclusive environment
- _____ Keeping the class sessions on track
- _____ Beginning and ending on time
- _____ Handling conflicting opinions with respect
- _____ Being prepared for class sessions

Scale: 1 - most negative, 10 - most positive

Please rate the physical setting for your group on the following using a scale of 1-10.

- _____ The space was free of distractions and interruptions
- _____ The space was physically comfortable and conductive to learning
- _____ The group could easily adjust to different configurations
- _____ It was easy to see instructional materials and group members
- _____ Restroom facilities were easily accessible
- _____ The space was accessible to those with disabilities

Do you have a particular faith tradition or spiritual orientation? If so, how would you name it?

[   ]

Did you feel that your opinions and perspective were respected in the following areas:

Course materials?	☐ Yes ☐ No
Class discussions?	☐ Yes ☐ No
By the group leader?	☐ Yes ☐ No

STUDENT EVALUATION

If you were an "informal student" (i.e., not a student seeking certification or CEUs), how much of the homework and reading did you complete? Please describe on a scale of 1-10, with 1 being virtually none and 10 being all of it.

_____

Did you do any of the Extra Mile assignments? ☐ Yes ☐ No

Scale: 1 - most negative, 10 - most positive

Please rate the quality of the homework assignments using a scale of 1-10.

_____ It was easy to understand the assignment

_____ The work could reasonably be completed between sessions

_____ I learned important things from doing the homework

_____ I did not feel pushed to come to a particular conclusion

Please answer the following questions:

Did you visit the Exploring the Bible Facebook page or follow us on Twitter @ExploreBible? Do you find these tools useful in staying connected to the Exploring the Bible community? Are there other ways you would prefer to be connected? If you would like to be on the Exploring the Bible e-mail list, please include your e-mail address in the space below.

Did this study answer any questions you had at the beginning? What were some of the most important questions that were answered for you?

STUDENT EVALUATION

Did anything disappoint you in this study? Was there something you expected that was not provided? Questions you really wanted answered that were not?

What new questions do you have upon completion that you did not have at the beginning? Do you find those new questions exciting or frustrating?

Did you learn anything of interest to you from this study? If you studied with a group, indicate how much of that came from the material provided and how much from the group discussion.

Have your impressions/beliefs/thoughts about the Bible changed as a result of this study? In what way?

STUDENT EVALUATION

Would you recommend this study to a friend?

How would you rate this study using a scale of 1-10, with 1 being not at all helpful and 10 being exceptionally helpful.

Other thoughts, comments, or suggestions?

Please return this evaluation to:
Massachusetts Bible Society, 199 Herrick Rd.,
Newton Centre, MA 02459
or e-mail to dsadmin@massbible.org.

Please return this evaluation to:
Massachusetts Bible Society, 199 Herrick Rd.,
Newton Centre, MA 02459
or e-mail to dsadmin@massbible.org.

FACILITATOR EVALUATION

Your Name: _____

Date the course began: _____

Date the course was completed: _____

Meeting location: _____

Course (circle one):   I   II   III

Respond to the following questions about the demographics of your group:

How many were in the group at the beginning?

How many were typically in attendance at any given session?

What ages were represented in your group?

Did any drop out? If so, did they give a reason?

What was the gender representation in your group?

Describe the racial/ethnic representation in your group:

FACILITATOR EVALUATION

Did you have group members who self-identified as being of no particular faith tradition other than Christian?

How many in your group were Extra Mile students?

Please comment about your class dynamics:

Did you feel adequately prepared to lead this group? Is there anything this guide or more training could have supplied to make the experience easier?

Scale: 1 - most negative, 10 - most positive

Please rate the Leader's Guide on the following using a scale of 1-10.

_____ The Leader's Guide was easy to understand and follow

_____ The class activities were appropriate to the session topic

_____ The class activities engaged the students in a positive way

_____ The class activities could be completed within the time allotted

_____ I always knew what to do in preparation for the next session

_____ I could fit preparation for sessions into my schedule easily

_____ The class flowed smoothly from beginning to end

_____ I was pleased with the overall quality of the Leader's Guide

FACILITATOR EVALUATION

Please respond to the following questions:

Did you encounter anything in class sessions that you felt unprepared to handle? If so, what?

To what extent did the students in your group know one another at the beginning of the course?

Did the group gain cohesion over the six sessions?

To what extent did the students do the homework and reading?

Did you personally enjoy facilitating this group? Why or why not? Would you do it again?

FACILITATOR EVALUATION

Other thoughts, comments, or suggestions?

Please return this evaluation to:
Massachusetts Bible Society, 199 Herrick Rd.,
Newton Centre, MA 02459
or e-mail to dsadmin@massbible.org.

Massachusetts Bible Society Statement on Scripture

The Massachusetts Bible Society is an ecumenical, Christian organization with a broad diversity of Scriptural approaches and interpretations among its members and supporters. The following statement on the nature of Scripture represents the guiding principle for our selection of programming and resources, but agreement with it is neither a pre-requisite for membership nor a litmus test for grant recipients.

> The Bible was written by many authors, all inspired by God. It is neither a simple collection of books written by human authors, nor is it the literal words of God dictated to human scribes. It is a source of religious truth, presented in a diversity of styles, genres, and languages and is not meant to serve as fact in science, history, or social structure.
>
> The Bible has authority for communities of faith who take time to study and prayerfully interpret its message, but it is also important for anyone who wants more fully to understand culture, religious thought, and the world in which we live.
>
> Biblical texts have been interpreted in diverse ways from generation to generation and are always filtered through the lens of the reader's faith and life experiences. This breadth and plurality, however, are what keep the Bible alive through the ages and enhance its ongoing, transformative power.

A Covenant for Bible Study

We covenant together to deal with our differences in a spirit of mutual respect and to refrain from actions that may harm the emotional and physical well-being of others.

The following principles will guide our actions:

- We will treat others whose views may differ from our own with the same courtesy we would want to receive ourselves.
- We will listen with a sincere desire to understand the point of view being expressed by another person, especially if it is different from our own.
- We will respect each other's ideas, feelings, and experiences.
- We will refrain from blaming or judging in our attitude and behavior towards others.
- We will communicate directly with any person with whom we may disagree in a respectful and constructive way.
- We will seek feedback to ensure that we have truly understood each other in our communications.

Additional agreements for our particular group:

Class Contact Information

Your Name: _____

Date the course began: _____

Date the course was completed: _____

Meeting location: _____

Please provide your preferred phone number and e-mail address.

Name	Phone	E-mail

Session 1: I Heard It In The Bible

Isaiah 40:15

Matthew 5:13

Genesis 3:3

Revelation 16:16

Ecclesiastes 10:1

Note: *For those using a pre-2010 edition of the New American Bible, the Ecclesiastes reference above is found in Ecclesiastes 9:18 instead of Ecclesiastes 10:1.*

Matthew 12:25

Matthew 15:14

Job 15:7

Job 19:20

1 Timothy 6:12

Matthew 5:41

Session 2: Stumbling Blocks

What do you think is the main point Paul is making in this chapter?

Paul is specifically addressing differences about early Christian behavior that arose from the culture of the first century C.E. Do you think his words would help or hinder people in conflict over what translation of the Bible should be used?

Can you think of other conflicts between people in our own day and age that could be helped by Paul's advice to the Romans?

Are there limitations to his advice or situations in which you believe the advice would not be helpful?

Sample Advertising Blurbs for What Is the Bible?

> Longer bulletin inserts, brochures, and/or posters can be supplied on request.

For Christian Audiences

How often have you thought, "I don't even know enough about the Bible to attend a Bible study—I'd be completely lost." What Is the Bible? is a small-group study made exactly for you. This study will help you to explore some of the best-known Bible passages and to discover some of the many ways that they can be interpreted. You will learn how the Bible as we know it was put together, who decided what parts were in and what parts were out, and where to go with your questions about the wonderful, baffling, beautiful, unsettling book we call the Bible.

What Is the Bible? will be offered [**provide your information here**]. Contact [**provide local contact**] to express your interest. The class can be taken either informally or to receive Continuing Education Units and/or eventual certification in biblical literacy.

To find out more please visit exploringthebible.org/faq.

For Mixed Audiences

Have you ever wondered what all the fuss is about the Bible? From classical art to modern politics to strange predictions about the end of the world, this ancient collection of texts and its characters are woven into the fabric of western civilization.

Exploring the Bible: The Dickinson Series is a series of three, six-week courses designed to teach (not preach) about the Bible and its contents. For people of all faiths or no faith, this educational series covers the bases from reading the most common stories and passages to learning the history and process behind the compilation of the Bible itself.

The first six-week study, What Is the Bible? is being offered [**provide local information**]. Contact [**provide local contact**] to express your interest. The class can be taken either informally or to receive Continuing Education Units and/or eventual certification in biblical literacy.

To find out more please visit exploringthebible.org/faq.

Glossary from Student Text

A.D.
Abbreviation for the Latin Anno Domini, meaning "in the year of the Lord." A system of notating time, generally used with B.C.

Antichrist
With a small "a" it is one who denies or opposes Christ. With a capital "A" it refers to a great antagonist expected to fill the world with wickedness but to be conquered forever by Christ at his second coming.

Apocalypse (adj. apocalyptic)
One of the Jewish and Christian writings of 200 B.C.E. to 150 C.E. marked by pseudonymity, symbolic imagery, and the expectation of an imminent cosmic cataclysm in which God destroys the ruling powers of evil and raises the righteous to life in a messianic kingdom.

Apocrypha
Books included in the Septuagint and Vulgate but excluded from the Jewish and Protestant canons of the Old Testament.

Ark
Something that affords protection and safety. Two different forms of this are prominent in the Bible. One is a boat—Noah's Ark—and the other is a sacred box—the Ark of the Covenant.

Babylonian Captivity (or Exile)
The period in Jewish history during which the Jews of the ancient Kingdom of Judah were captives in Babylon—conventionally 586–538 B.C.E. although some claim a date of 596 B.C.E.

B.C.
Abbreviation for "Before Christ." A system of notating time, generally used with A.D.

B.C.E.
Abbreviation for "Before the Christian Era" or "Before the Common Era." An academic and faith-neutral notation of time. Generally used with C.E.

Canon
An authoritative list of books accepted as Holy Scripture. The word is from the Latin meaning "rule" or "standard."

Catholic
With a small "c," the word means "universal." It is used this way in the Apostles' Creed. With a capital "C" the word denotes the Roman Catholic Church.

A B **C** D E F G H I J K L M N O P Q R S T U V W X Y Z

C.E.
Abbreviation for "Christian Era" or "Common Era." An academic and faith-neutral notation of time. Generally used with B.C.E.

Codex
A manuscript book especially of Scripture, classics, or ancient annals. A codex is bound like we are used to in a modern book instead of the more common scroll.

Codex Sinaiticus
A fourth-century, hand-written copy of the Greek Bible.

Concordance
An alphabetical index of all the words in a text or corpus of texts, showing every contextual occurrence of a word.

Conquest
The period of Jewish history described in the biblical book of Joshua. Many scholars believe the settlement of the Hebrews in Canaan took place over a much longer period of time and with less bloodshed than is depicted in Joshua. They would say that there was no actual "conquest" at all.

Covenant
A formal, solemn, and binding agreement.

Creationism
The doctrine or theory holding that matter, the various forms of life, and the world were created by God out of nothing in a way determined by a literal reading of Genesis.

Deuterocanonical
Of, relating to, or constituting the books of Scripture contained in the Septuagint but not in the Hebrew canon. Primarily Roman Catholic and Orthodox usage for the texts known to Jews and Protestants as the Apocrypha.

Diaspora
A scattered population originating from a single area. In this course the word refers specifically to Jews living outside of Israel.

Dispensationalism
A system of Christian belief, formalized in the nineteenth century, that divides human history into seven distinct ages or dispensations.

Evangelical
When used with a capital "E," this refers to those in Christian traditions that emphasize a high view of biblical authority, the need for personal relationship with God achieved through a conversion experience (being "born again"), and an emphasis on sharing the gospel that Jesus' death and resurrection save us from our sins. The tradition generally deemphasizes ritual and prioritizes personal experience.

Gilgamesh
A Sumerian king and hero of the Epic of Gilgamesh, which contains a story of a great flood during which a man is saved in a boat.

Hapax Legomenon (pl. Hapax Legomena)
A word or form of speech occurring only once in a document or body of work.

Hasmonean Dynasty
Those who ruled Judea in the late second century B.C.E. This represented a brief period of independence between the occupying forces of Greece and Rome and is described in the books of the Maccabees.

Hyksos
Of or relating to a Semitic dynasty that ruled Egypt from about the eighteenth to the sixteenth centuries B.C.E.

Inerrancy
Exemption from error. Infallibility.

Jerome
(ca. 347 C.E.–30 September 420 C.E.) A Roman Christian priest, confessor, theologian, and historian, who became a Doctor of the Church. Best known for his translation of the Bible into Latin (the Vulgate). Recognized by the Roman Catholic and Eastern Orthodox churches as a saint.

LXX
See Septuagint.

Mainline
Certain Protestant churches in the United States that comprised a majority of Americans from the colonial era until the early twentieth century. The group is contrasted with evangelical and fundamentalist groups. They include Congregationalists, Episcopalians, Methodists, northern Baptists, most Lutherans, and most Presbyterians, as well as some smaller denominations.

Marcion (of Sinope)
(ca. 85–160 C.E.) An early Christian bishop who believed the God of the Hebrew Scriptures to be inferior or subjugated to the God of the New Testament and developed his own canon of Scripture accordingly. He was excommunicated for his belief.

Masoretes
Groups of Jewish scribes working between the seventh and eleventh centuries C.E. They added vowel notations to the Hebrew Scriptures.

Mordecai Nathan (Rabbi)
Philosopher rabbi of the fifteenth century C.E. who wrote the first concordance to the Hebrew Bible and added numbered verse notations to the Hebrew Bible for the first time.

Orthodox
With a capital "O" referring to the Eastern Orthodox Church (and its various geographic subdivisions), the Oriental Orthodox churches (and their subdivisions), and any Western Rite Orthodox congregations allied with the above.

Ossuary
A depository, most commonly a box, for the bones (as opposed to the entire corpse) of the dead.

Pentateuch
The first five books of the Bible: Genesis, Exodus, Leviticus, Numbers, and Deuteronomy.

Pharisee
A member of a segment of Judaism of the inter-testamental period noted for strict observance of rites and ceremonies of the written law and for insistence on the validity of their own oral traditions concerning the law.

Protestant
Used here in the broadest sense of any Christian not of a Catholic or Orthodox church.

Pseudepigrapha
In biblical studies, the Pseudepigrapha are Jewish religious works written ca. 200 B.C.E.–200 C.E., which are not part of the canon of any established Jewish or Christian tradition.

Rapture
The term "rapture" is used in at least two senses in modern traditions of Christian theology: in pre-tribulationist views, in which a group of people will be "left behind," and as a synonym for the final resurrection generally.

Robert Stephanus
Protestant book printer living in France in the sixteenth century who divided the chapters of the New Testament into the verses we have today.

Septuagint or LXX
An ancient Greek translation of the Hebrew Scriptures. Translation began in the third century B.C.E. with the Pentateuch and continued for several centuries.

Stephen Langton
Theology professor in Paris and archbishop of Canterbury in the thirteenth century who first added chapter divisions to the Bible.

Supersessionism
The idea that God's covenant with Christians supersedes and therefore displaces God's covenant with Israel.

Synoptic Gospels
From the Greek meaning to "see alike," the Synoptics are Matthew, Mark, and Luke.

Testament
With a capital "T" it means either of the two main divisions of the Bible: the Old Testament or the New Testament. With a small "t" the word simply means a covenant or agreement that is formalized in writing and witnessed.

Tetragrammaton
The four consonants in Exodus 3:14 (YHWH) that comprise God's name.

Vulgate
The late fourth-century Latin translation of the Bible done by St. Jerome.

THE **IDEAL DVD PAIRING** FOR

Exploring the Bible

Produced by the Massachusetts Bible Society and The Walker Group, LLC, the 28-minute video **One Book, Many Voices** will let you hear directly from scholars, clergy, and just regular folks helping you to reflect on these questions:

- **How do YOU understand the Bible?**
- **Can we trust what is in the Bible?**
- **Is there a right or wrong way to read it?**

To view the trailer and/or order a physical copy of the DVD, go to **massbible.org/DVD**. To buy or rent a streaming download, either search amazon.com for "One Book, Many Voices" or scan the QR code with your smart phone.

Help More People Explore the Bible

Your gift of $25, $50, $100, or more supports *Exploring the Bible* scholarships, study Bibles for those in need, and helps keep our training events at a reasonable cost.

$ _____

○ One-Time Donation   ○ Recurring

_____
Name

_____
Address

_____
Phone

_____
Email

○ Check Enclosed

_____
Credit Card Number

_____   _____
Expiration Date   Security Code

Mail this completed form to:
Massachusetts Bible Society
199 Herrick Rd., Newton Centre, MA 02459

You can also donate by calling 617.969.9404, by e-mail at dsadmin@massbible.org, or online at exploringthebible.org.

www.ingramcontent.com/pod-product-compliance
Lightning Source LLC
Chambersburg PA
CBHW080444110426
42743CB00016B/3268